D1490012

MOOD RIVER

ORGANIZED BY JEFFREY KIPNIS AND ANNETTA MASSIE
WITH AMY SCHMERSAL, JOBY POTTMEYER, AND RUJUTA MODY
CONTRIBUTIONS BY SHERRI GELDIN, SANFORD KWINTER,
SYLVIA LAVIN, CHEE PEARLMAN, JOSE OUBRERIE
AND A FOREWORD BY PHILIP JOHNSON

PRODUCED IN ASSOCIATION WITH THE EXHIBITION
MOOD RIVER
FEBRUARY 3–MAY 26, 2002
WEXNER CENTER FOR THE ARTS
THE OHIO STATE UNIVERSITY
COLUMBUS, OHIO

THE EXHIBITION IS MADE POSSIBLE BY A GENEROUS LEAD GIFT FROM BATTELLE.

MAJOR SUPPORT IS PROVIDED BY PETER B. LEWIS, AGNES GUND AND
DANIEL SHAPIRO, ACCENTURE, AND SHISEIDO CO., LTD.

ADDITIONAL SUPPORT IS PROVIDED BY THE NATIONAL ENDOWMENT FOR THE ARTS, THE OHIO ARTS COUNCIL,
THE OHIO STATE UNIVERSITY DIVISION OF STUDENT AFFAIRS, COCA-COLA, AND THE CORPORATE ANNUAL FUND
OF THE WEXNER CENTER FOUNDATION. *PROMOTIONAL SUPPORT IS PROVIDED BY* WBNS 10TV.

MOOD RIVER INCLUDES FREE BASIN AND DESIGN AFOOT: ATHLETIC SHOES 1995–2000.
FREE BASIN IS A PROJECT BY SIMPARCH *IN COLLABORATION WITH* PETER ENG, PAT FINLAY, CHRIS VORHEES,
AND HAMZA WALKER. *IT WAS ORGANIZED FOR* THE HYDE PARK ART CENTER OF CHICAGO *BY* LIA ALEXOPOULOS
AND SPONSORED BY MESA DEVELOPMENT CORPORATION. *DESIGN AFOOT WAS ORGANIZED BY* THE
SAN FRANCISCO MUSEUM OF MODERN ART.

GRAPHIC DESIGN
WORK IN PROGRESS
PATRICK LI
VICSON GUEVARA
EDITOR
ANN BREMNER
RYAN SHAFER

PUBLISHED BY
WEXNER CENTER FOR THE ARTS
THE OHIO STATE UNIVERSITY
1871 NORTH HIGH STREET
COLUMBUS, OHIO 43210-1393
614-292-0330
WWW.WEXARTS.ORG

ISBN: 1-881390-30-6
DISTRIBUTED BY DISTRIBUTED ART PUBLISHERS, NEW YORK 800-338-2665
WEXNER CENTER FOR THE ARTS, THE OHIO STATE UNIVERSITY
COLUMBUS, OHIO
2002

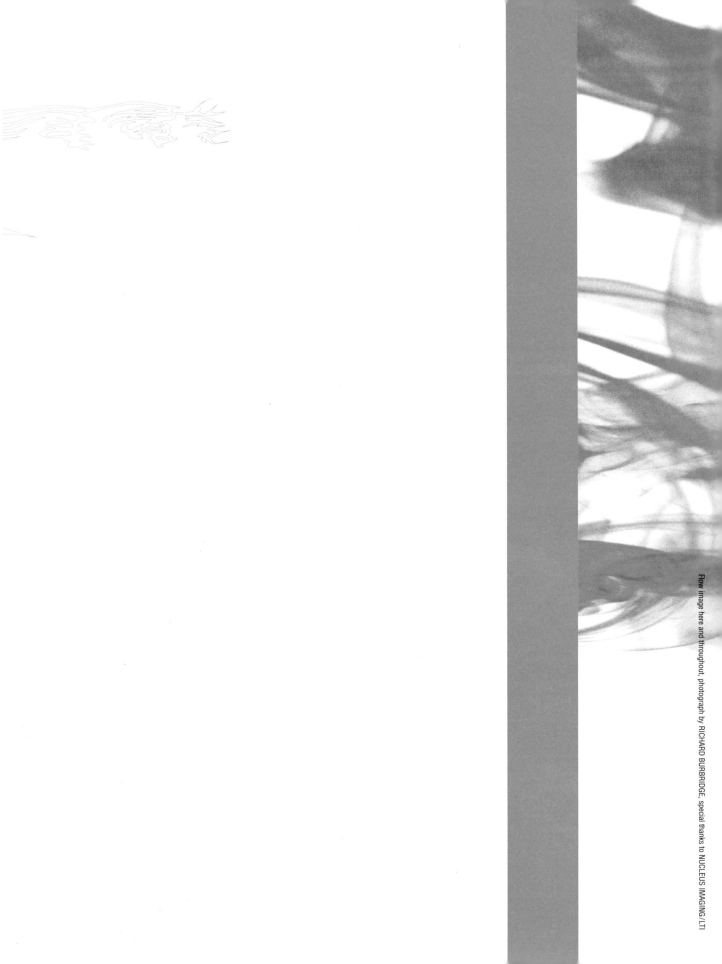

Flow image here and throughout, photograph by RICHARD BURBRIDGE, special thanks to NUCLEUS IMAGING/LTI

CONTENTS

PLAZA: Enron Wind, Wind turbine blade, Courtesy of the City of Storm Lake, Iowa, and the Storm Lake Chamber of Commerce GALLERY RAMP: *Collection of Bread Ties,* Ben Nicholson Collection, *Museum of Airline Plastic,* Chee Pearlman Collection GALLERY A: Siobhán Hapaska, *Hanker,* 1997, Fiberglass, polyester gel coat, blue LED, 57 x 86½ x 19¾", Courtesy of Anthony Podesta, Washington, D.C., *Land,* 1998, Fiberglass, acrylic paint, two-pack acrylic lacquer, magnets, water, air plants, 37 x 94 x 52", Courtesy of Anthony Podesta, Washington, D.C., Enlai Hooi, *Foldings,* Paper, Variable dimensions, Courtesy of Enlai Hooi, *Pendant Lamps,* Paper and electrical fixtures, 36 x 36 x 36" (approx.), Courtesy of Enlai Hooi, *Shell Screen Panels,* 3 screen panels and lights, Variable dimensions, Courtesy of Enlai Hooi, Rachael Neubauer, *Mist,* 2000, Polystyrene foam, epoxy, and lacquer, 7 x 24 x 6 1/2", Private collection, San Francisco, *Pearl Essence,* 2000, Polysterene foam, epoxy, and lacquer, 24 x 30 x 7", San Francisco Museum of Modern Art, Purchased through a gift of Nelcy Tarics, Alessi, *Babyboop,* 2000, Designer: Ron Arad, Courtesy of Museo Alessi, Aliantedizioni: *W Plate,* 2000, Designer: Alessandro Loschiavo, *Giava,* 2001, Designer: Makoto Kawamoto, Both courtesy of Aliantedizioni, Artemide, *Boalum Lamp,* Designer: Livio Castiglioni, *Brezza Sospensione,* Designer: Andrea Anastasio, Both courtesy of Artemide, Blu Dot, *Perf Magazine Rack,* 1996, Designers: John Christakos, Charlie Lazor, Maurice Blanks, Courtesy of Blu Dot, Hussein Chalayan, *Airmail Dress,* Designer: Hussein Chalayan, *Layer Dress, Geotropics* Collection, Spring/Summer 1999, Designer: Hussein Chalayan, Both courtesy of Hussein Chalayan, Ane Christensen, *Cracked Bowl,* 2000, Designer: Ane Christensen, Courtesy of Ane Christensen, CP Company, Transformables: *Tenda,* 2000, Courtesy of CP Company, Danese Milano, *Antipodi,* 1990, Designer: Marco Ferreri, Courtesy of Danese Milano, Foscarini USA, *Coco,* Designer: Aldo Cibic, Courtesy of Foscarini USA, Hopf + Wortmann, *Liquid_Light Drop_1 ceiling,* 2000, *Liquid_Light Drop_3,* 2000, *Liquid_Light Drop_4,* 2000, *Liquid_Light Drop_ pendulum,* 2000, All designer: Hopf + Wortmann, All courtesy of Hopf + Wortmann, Munich, Kartell, *Portariviste,* Designer: Giotto Stoppino, Courtesy of Kartell, Korban/Flaubert, *Knot Lamp,* Designers: Janos Korban, Stefanie Flaubert, Courtesy of Korban/Flaubert, Harri Koshinen, *Block Lamp,* Designer: Harri Koskinen, Greg Lynn, Shelving system, Designer: Greg Lynn, Courtesy of Greg Lynn, Mathmos Ltd, *Bubble,* Designer: Aaron Rincover, Courtesy of Mathmos Ltd, Polyline, *Folder Chair,* 2000, Designer: Stefan Schöning, Courtesy of Polyline, Sarah Schwartz, *Perfect Veil,* Designer: Sarah Schwartz, Courtesy of Sarah Schwartz, Servo, *Thermo-Cline,* 2001, Courtesy of Servo, Snowcrash, *Globlow,* 1998, Designers: Vesa Hinkola, Marcus Nevalainen, Rane Vaskivuori, Courtesy of Snowcrash, Stone Island, *Serie 100 Knit,* Courtesy of Stone Island, Tony Stuart, *Veil,* Designer: Tony Stuart, Courtesy of Tony Stuart, Ansel Thompson, *Chair #1,* 2001, Designer: Ansel Thompson, Courtesy of Ansel Thompson, Tiffany & Co., *Bean* minaudière (evening bag), 1974 (production begun), Designer: Elsa Peretti for Tiffany & Co., Courtesy of Tiffany & Co., New York GALLERY B: Acura, Acura *3.2 CL* taillight, 2001, Acura *3.2 TL-S* taillight, 2001, Acura RSX taillight, 2001, All courtesy of Lindsay Acura, AdHoc Entwicklung and Vertrieb GmbH, *Cerastar Ceramic Knives,* Designer: Peter Valentin, *Storm Lantern Lighters,* Both courtesy of AdHoc Entwicklung and Vertrieb GmbH, Agape SRL, *Gerba Soap Dispensors,* 1999, Designers: F. Bortolani, E. Righi, Courtesy of Agape SRL, Alessi, *Walter Wayle II,* 1990, Designer: Philippe Starck, *Parmenide,* 1994, Designer: Alejandro Ruiz, *Nonno di Antonio,* 1996, Designer: Guido Venturini, *Dr. Kiss,* 1998, Designer: Philippe Starck, *Dr. Kleen,* 1998, Designer: Philippe Starck, *Dr. Spoon,* 1998, Designer: Philippe Starck, *Moosk,* 1998, Designer: Philippe Starck, *Punta d'argento,* 1998, Designer: Massimo Scolari, *Segnalibro,* 1998, Designer: Massimo Scolari, *Big Bubbles,* 1999, Designer: Stefano Giovannoni, *Stavros,* 1999, Designer: Marc Newson, *Canaglia,* 2000, Designer: Stefano Pirovano, *Gnam,* 2000, Designers: Stefano Giovannoni, Elisa Gargan, *Splügen,* 2001, Designer: Achille Castiglioni, *Ali-the-gator,* 2001, Designer: Khodi Feiz, All courtesy of Museo Alessi, Apple Computer, Inc., *iMac Pro Mouse,* Courtesy of Apple Computer, Inc., Applied Concepts, *Robohammer,* Courtesy of Applied Concepts, Artemide, E.light, Designer: Ernesto Gismondi, Courtesy of Artemide, Artitudes Designs, *Big Foot Razor,* Designer: Eric Nanson, Courtesy of Artitudes Designs, Bang & Olufsen, *Beocom 1401, Beocom 1600, Beocom 2500, Beocom 6000, BeoTalk 1200,* All courtesy of Bang & Olufsen, Becton Dickinson, *Safety Glide,* Courtesy of Becton Dickinson, Bell Sports, *Aquila, Ghisallo, Influx, Ukon,* All courtesy of Bell Sports, BOLT, *East3 Thoughtcaster,* 2000, Courtesy of BOLT, Brookstone Company, *Ergonomic Flashlight,* Courtesy of Brookstone Company, Cadillac, Cadillac *Deville* taillights, 2001, Courtesy of Immke Crestview Cadillac, Calligrane, White pencils, Caran d'Ache of Switzerland, Ballpoint pen, Courtesy of Caran d'Ache of Switzerland, Casabella, *Curvaceous Bowl Brush, Curvaceous Ergo Broom,* Both courtesy of Casabella, Chevrolet, Chevrolet *Monte Carlo* headlight, 2000, Courtesy of Byers Dublin Dodge, Chrysler, Chrysler *Concorde* taillight, 2001, Chrysler *PT Cruiser* taillight, 2001, Chrysler *Sebring* taillight, 2001, All courtesy of Byers Dublin Dodge, Colgate Palmolive, Various toothbrushes, Courtesy of Colgate Palmolive, Colibri, *Electro-Quartz Eclipse, Quantum Eliminator, Quantum Talon, Quantum Translucent Windjammer,* All courtesy of Colibri, Crest, Various toothbrushes, A. T. Cross Company, *Ion Pen,* 2001, Gel-pen refills (for *Ion*), Both courtesy of the A. T. Cross Company, Danese Milano, *Benbecula,* 1961, Designer: Enzo Mari, *Ameland,* 1962, Designer: Enzo Mari, Both courtesy of Danese Milano, Dodge, Dodge *Avenger* taillight, 1998, Dodge *Venom/Viper* headlight, 2001, Both courtesy of Byers Dublin Dodge, Donna Karan Cosmetics, *Cashmere Mist Eau de Toilette Spray, DKNY Men's Fragrance, Eau de Toilette, Donna Karan New York Eau de Parfum Spray/ Vaporisateur,* All courtesy of Donna Karan Cosmetics, Dornbracht GmbH, *Bellevue, Domani, Fino, 2000, Giorno,* Designer: Massimo Iosa Ghini, All courtesy of Dornbracht GmbH, Iserlohn, Germany, Dyson Ltd, *Dyson DC05 Dual Cyclone Vacuum Cleaner,* Designer: James Dyson, *Dyson DC07 Root Cyclone Vacuum Cleaner,* Designer: James Dyson, Both courtesy of Dyson Ltd, Ethentica, *Ethenticator USB 2500,* Courtesy of Ethentica, Euro-Pro Corporation, *Euro-Pro Shark Hand Held Vacuum,* Courtesy of the Euro-Pro Corporation, Fisher-Price, *View-Master Virtual Viewer,* Courtesy of Fisher-Price, Fiskars Consumer Products, Inc., *FISKARS® Classic Pro Bypass Pruner (#7938), FISKARS® PowerGear® Bypass Pruner (#7936), FISKARS® Ratchet Anvil Pruner (#7685), FISKARS® Softouch® Serrated Floral Snip (#9931), No. 8 Softgrip® Pinking Shears (#9881-7097), Sliding Blade PowerTooth™ Pruning Saw with Belt Clip (#9259), Softouch® Pinking Shears (#99157097), Softouch® 65mm Rotary Cutter (#9544-7097),* All courtesy of Fiskars Consumer Products, Inc., Fluocaril, *Stylic,* Ford, Ford *Escort* taillight, 1999, Ford *Focus ZX3* taillight, 2000, Ford *Taurus* taillight, 2001, All courtesy of Germain Toyota, Forms+Surfaces, *The Wave Collection,* 1997, Designer: Will

Prindle, *Meridian* doorpulls, 2000, Designer: Tom Peters, Both courtesy of Forms+Surfaces, The Gillette Company, *Mach 3, Venus,* Both courtesy of The Gillette Company, Giro, *Eclipse, Pneumo, Switchblade, Torrent,* All courtesy of Bell Sports, GlaxoSmithKline, Various Aquafresh toothbrushes, Courtesy of GlaxoSmithKline, Global, Fishbone tweezers, 4 pc. steak knife set, Designer: Mino Tsuchida, Various knives and utensils, Designer: Komin Yamada, All courtesy of Sointu USA Incorporated, Guzzini, Blender, Designer: Dario Tanfoglio, Bottle opener, Designer: Ross Lovegrove, Can opener, Designer: Ross Lovegrove, Dishrack, Designer: Bruno Gecchelin, Electonic gas lighter, Designer: Ross Lovegrove, Garlic press, Designer: Ross Lovegrove, *Mikado* flatware, Designer: Dario Tanfoglio, Nutcracker, Designer: Ross Lovegrove, Potato peeler, Designer: Ross Lovegrove, *The Stone CD Holder,* Designer: Enzo Calabrese, All courtesy of Fratelli Guzzini, Hackman Tools, *Citterio Collective Tools,* 2000, Designer: Antonio Citterio, *Koskinen 2000,* Designer: Harri Koskinen, Lovegrove 2000, Designer: Ross Lovegrove, All courtesy of Designor OyAb, Hackman Tools Helsinki, Finland, Hammacher Schlemmer, Hand-held vacuum, Ice Blades, *Modular Weather Station, On the Go Cordless Iron and Steamer, Ultimate At-Home Groomer, Unbreakable No-battery Bulbless Flashlight,* All courtesy of Hammacher Schlemmer, Hitachi Power Tools, *CR24DV Reciprocating Saw,* Courtesy of Hitachi Power Tools, Hold Everything, Black pencils, Honda, Honda *Civic* headlight, 2001, Courtesy of Immke Crestview Cadillac, Hyundai, Hyundai *Elantra GLS* taillight, 2000, Courtesy of Dennis Mitsubishi Inc, Interdesign USA, *Squeegee La Racloir,* ISI North America, *Deos Millenium, Elios Ergogrip Peeler, Elios Julienne Peeler, Krab Bottle Opener, Oros Citrus Peeler,* All courtesy of ISI North America, Issey Miyake, *L'Eau d'Issey, Le Feu d'Issey, Le Feu d'Issey Light, Soleil d'Issey,* All courtesy of Beauté Prestige International, Jaguar, Jaguar *XK8,* headlight and taillight, 2001, Courtesy of Byers Imports on Hamilton, Jorg Hysek, *Lacquer,* Courtesy of Jorg Hysek, Kia, Kia *Rio* headlight and taillight, 2001, Courtesy of James Gill at Chesrown Oldsmobile GMC, KIA, Kikkerland, *Eddy Ballpoint, Object Ballpoint, Shark Ballpoint,* Short stainless shoehorn, Travel alarm/torch, Travel lint brush, Travel shoehorn, *Twist Ballpoint,* All courtesy of Kikkerland, Koziol Geschenkartikel GmbH, *Elise the Watering Can,* Courtesy of Koziol Geschenkartikel GmbH, Lamborghini, Lamborghini *Diablo 6.0* taillight, 2001, Courtesy of Nelson Auto Group, L'Equip, *L'Equip Juicer,* Designer: James Pascotti, Courtesy of L'Equip, Lexon (Zona Alta Projects), *Katana* letter opener, 2000, Designer: Takashi Kato, Courtesy of Lexon, distributed by Zona Alta Projects, Lexus, Lexus *GS430* taillight,

2001, Courtesy of Germain Toyota, Luminair, Inc., *Neon Night Light,* Courtesy of Luminair, Inc., Marutomi, *Capri,* Designer: Massimo Morozzi, *Elba,* Designer: Massimo Morozzi, *Ischia,* Designer: Massimo Morozzi, All courtesy of Marutomi, Mazda, Mazda *Miata* taillight, 2001, Mazda *Tribute* headlight, 2001, Both courtesy of Byers Dublin Dodge, Mercedes-Benz, Mercedes *CLK 500* headlight, 2001, Courtesy of Ed Potter, Inc, Metrokane, *Rabbit Corkscrew,* Designer: Edward Kilduff, Courtesy of Metrokane, Mitsubishi, Mitsubishi *Eclipse Spyder* taillight, 1999, Mitsubishi *Eclipse GS* taillight, 2000, Mitsubishi *Eclipse* taillight, 2001, All courtesy of Byers Dublin Dodge, Mono Tabletop, Bottle opener, Designer: Wolfgang Dufhues, *Citro* orange peeler, Designer: Markus Brodmerkel, *Filio* egg cup sets, flatware, and party set, Designer: Ralph Krämer, *Piccino* servers, Designer: Ralph Krämer, *Pick Up 2 Party Servers,* Designer: Markus Brodmerkel, *Pico* walnut opener, Designer: Ralph Krämer, Salad serving set, Designer: Ralph Krämer, Various *Zeug* knives and flatware, Designer: Michael Schneider, All courtesy of Mono Tabletop, Oldsmobile, Oldsmobile *Aurora* taillight, 2001, Courtesy of James Gill at Chesrown Oldsmobile, GMC, KIA, Oral B, Various Oral B toothbrushes, Courtesy of The Gillette Company, OrangeX, *OrangeX Ojex Manual Juicer,* Designer: Smart Design LLC, Courtesy of OrangeX, OXO International, Various *OXO Good Grips* household utensils, Various *OXO Good Grips* kitchen utensils, Various *OXO Good Grips* utility brushes, All courtesy of OXO International, Parks Products, *Grundig Avantgarde Pro 8875,* Courtesy of Parks Products, Parogencyl, *Serena,* Pentech, *Softtech,* Pentel, *Milky Gel Roller,* Pfizer Consumer Group, Schick *Protector* razor, Schick *Silk Effects+* razor, Pilot, *Dr. Grip Neon, Easy Touch, Easy Touch Retractable,* Polaroid, *i-Zone Instant Pocket Camera,* Changeable faceplates for *Convertible i-Zone Camera,* Pontiac, Pontiac *Bonneville* taillight and headlight, 2001, Pontiac *FireBird* taillight, 2001, Pontiac *Grand Am* taillight, 2001, Pontiac *Grand Prix* taillight, 2001, All courtesy of Dave Gill Pontiac-GMC, Porsche, Porsche *Boxster* headlight and taillight, 2001, Porsche *911 Carrera* taillight, 2001, Both courtesy of MidWestern Auto Group, Rosendahl A/S, Flyswatter, Designer: Erik Bagger, Ice scraper, Designer: Erik Bagger, Razor, Designer: Flemming Bo Hansen, Wallpaper magazine rack, Designer: Maria Berntsen, All courtesy of Rosendahl A/S, Denmark, Rotring, *Core: Coridium, Core: Eternium, Core: Lysium, Core: Technor, Initial, Quattro Data Pen,* All courtesy of Sanford Corporation, Salter Housewares, *Bathroom Scales-9981 Digital Glass Scales,* Courtesy of Salter Housewares, Sensa by Willat, *City Lights Collection, Classic Collection, Hamptons Collection, Metal Collection, The Minx Collection, Minxlink Collection, Platinum Minx,* Designer: Boyd Willat, All courtesy of Sensa by Willat, SheafferPen, *ErgoPen,* Designer: Charles Debbas, Courtesy of SheafferPen, Division of Bic USA Inc., Shiseido, *Zen,* Courtesy of Shiseido, Smith & Hawken, *Swiss Felco Pruners, Double Grip Pruners,* Both courtesy of Smith & Hawken, Swingline, *Anywhere Stapler, Heavy Duty Staple Remover, Premium Spoon Remover, Smooth Grip Desk Stapler, Soft Grip Stapler, TOT Grip Stapler,* All courtesy of Swingline, a division of ACCO Brands Inc, Timothy Grannis Studios, *The Wallet Pen,* Designer: Timothy Grannis, Courtesy of Timothy Grannis, Tombow, *Mono Adhesive, Mono Correction Tape, Object, Zoom 707, Zoom 980,* All courtesy of Tombow, Toyota, Toyota *Echo* taillight, 2000, Toyota *Camry* taillight, 2001, Toyota *Solaris* taillight, 2001, All courtesy of Germain Toyota, Tripod Design, *Handy Wormy,* Designer: Satoshi Nakagawa, *Wing Finger Dancer,* Designer: Satoshi Nakagawa, Both courtesy of Tripod Design, Troika, Various pens, *James Bond Monocular, Ovum* bottle opener, *Shark* letter opener, *Sudden Death* flyswatter, Unilever Home and Personal Care, Various Mentadent toothbrushes, Courtesy of Unilever Home and Personal Care, Valli & Valli, Cabinet hardware: A 291, Designer: Itamar Harari, A 289, Designer: Giancarlo Vegni, A 243, A 234, A 235, A 236, A 240, A 241, A 246, A 252, A 256, A 266, A 278, A 284, Designer: Eero Aarnio, A 262, Designer: Alan Gordon Morris, A 243, A 250, Designer: Gost & Schreyer, A 238, A 244, Designer: Cozza e Mascheroni, A 230, A 231, Designer: Studio Forges, Cabinet knobs: B 247, Designer: Studio Forges, B 241, B 243, Designer: Eero Aarnio, Door levers: H 338, Designer: Yoshimi Kono, H 337, Designer: Gustav Peichl, H 335, Designer: Richard Meier, H 328, H 334, Designer: Foster and Partners, H 333, Designer: Piano Design Workshop, H 330, Designer: Matteo Thun, H 326, Designer: Antonio Citterio, H 322, Designer: Cini Boeri, H 315, Designer: Pierluigi Cerri, H 314, Designer: Sottsass Associati, All courtesy of Valli & Valli USA Inc, Vitry, Cuticle

trimmer, Pumice stone, Watermark Designs, *Cascade, Italia, Milano,* All courtesy of Watermark Designs, Wiss, *Ergonomic Shears,* Designer: David Chapin, Courtesy of Wiss, xO, *POAA,* 1999, Designer: Philippe Starck, Courtesy of xO
GALLERY B/C: Alias Spa, *Armframe,* 1994, Designer: Alberto Meda, *Longframe,* 1994, Designer: Alberto Meda, Both courtesy of Alias Spa, Ron Arad, *Narrow Paparadelle,* 1992, Designer: Ron Arad, Courtesy of the Museum of Fine Arts, Houston, Bernhardt Design, *Go Chair,* Designer: Ross Lovegrove, Courtesy of Bernhardt Design, Blu Dot, *Detroit Cocktail Table,* 1996, Designers: John Christakos, Charlie Lazor, Maurice Blanks, Courtesy of Blu Dot, Bluesquare, *Polar Chair,* Designer: Matthew Butler, *Profile Chair,* Designer: Matthew Butler, Both courtesy of Bluesquare, Boum Design, *Air Chair,* Designer: Pierre Bougeunnec, *Air Lounge Chair,* Designer: Pierre Bougeunnec, Both courtesy of Boum Design, Brown Jordan, *Aero Arm Chair,* September 1998, Designer: Richard Frinier, *Nxt Arm Chair,* September 2000, Designer: Richard Frinier, Both courtesy of Brown Jordan, Edra Spa, *Anemone Chair,* Designer: Fernando and Humberto Campana, *Meditation Pod,* 2001, Designer: Steven Blaess, *Pororoca,* 2001, Designer: Flavia Alves de Souza, *Pororoca* (stool), 2001, Designer: Flavia Alves de Souza, *Zig Zag Paravento Screen,* 2001, Designer: Fernando and Humberto Campana, All courtesy of Edra Spa, Foundation 33, *Flange Chair,* Designers: Daniel Eatock & Sam Solhaug, Courtesy of Foundation 33, Hopf + Wortmann, *Leni,* 2000, Designer: Hopf + Wortmann, Courtesy of Hopf + Wortmann, Munich, Kartell, *Bubble Club Chair,* Designer: Philippe Starck, *Bubble Club Couch,* Designer: Philippe Starck, *FPE Stackable Chair,* Designer: Ron Arad, *La Marie Chair,* Designer: Philippe Starck, *LCP Spring Chair,* Designer: Martin van Severen, All courtesy of Kartell, Korban/Flaubert, *Membrane Chaise,* Designers: Janos Korban, Stefanie Flaubert, Courtesy of Korban/Flaubert, Moorhead & Moorhead, *Polypropylene Chair Low,* 2001, Designer: Moorhead & Moorhead, Courtesy of Moorhead & Moorhead, OCEAN North, *Extraterrain,* 1995, Designer: Kivi Sotamaa, Courtesy of Kivi Sotamaa and Markus Holmsten, Giovanni Pagnotta, *Z,* Designer: Giovanni Pagnotta, Courtesy of Giovanni Pagnotta, R+D Design, *Worm Bench,* 2000, Designer: Michael Ryan, Courtesy of R+D Design, Karim Rashid, *Blob Chair,* 1999, Designer: Karim Rashid, Courtesy of Karim Rashid, The Terence Conran Shop, *GhostHome,* Designer: Jean Marie Massaud, Courtesy of The Terence Conran Shop, Terminal-NYC, *Z Computer Chair,* 2001, Designer: Yilmaz Zenger, Distributed by Terminal-NYC, VISA VERSA, *Lounge, Pouf, Quattro, Solo,* All designers: Quinze & Milan, All courtesy of VISA VERSA, Vitra, Inc, *Panton Chair,* 2000, Designer: Verner Panton, *W. W. Stool,* 1991, Designer: Philippe Starck, Both courtesy of Vitra, Inc
GALLERY C: John Chamberlain, *Rubber Comedy,* 2001, Painted and chromed steel, 38⅛ x 52⅛ x 45½", Courtesy of PaceWildenstein, New York, Tony Cragg, *Clear Glass Stack,* 1999, Glass, 86½ x 51¼ x 55⅛", Courtesy Büro Anthony Cragg, E. V. Day, *Bombshell,* 1999, Dress, monofilament and turnbuckles, 192 x 240 x 240", Courtesy of The Saatchi Gallery, London, Frank Gehry, *Horse's Head,* 2000, Fiberglass, 26 x 41 x 60", Courtesy of Gehry Partners, David Reed, Selected new paintings, Courtesy of Max Protetch Gallery, Frank Stella, *Untitled (Airport Study),* Metal, sintra plastic, 30 x 45 x 18", Courtesy of Frank Stella, *Untitled,* Sintra plastic, 9 x 6 x 6", Courtesy of Frank Stella, Aeromax, *Lakota Wind Turbine,* Courtesy of Aeromax, Agape SRL, *Foglio,* Designer: Benidini Associati, Courtesy of Agape SRL, Apple Computer, Inc, *iBook, iMac, iMac Pro Keyboard, Macintosh Airport Internet Station,* All courtesy of Apple Computer, Inc., Becton Dickinson, *Safety Glide,* Courtesy of Becton Dickinson, Calligrane, White pencils, Hussein Chalayan, *Fin Top, Before Minus Now* Collection, Spring/Summer 2000, Designer: Hussein Chalayan, *Gathered Skirt, Before Minus Now* Collection, Spring/Summer 2000, Designer: Hussein Chalayan, *Pink Tulle Dress #2, Before Minus Now* Collection, Spring/Summer 2000, Designer: Hussein Chalayan, *Underskirt, Before Minus Now* Collection, Spring/Summer 2000, Designer: Hussein Chalayan, *Fin Pleat Top, Afterwords* Collection, Autumn/Winter 2000, Designer: Hussein Chalayan, *Topiary Dress, Afterwords* Collection, Autumn/Winter 2000, Designer: Hussein Chalayan, All courtesy of Hussein Chalayan, *Table Skirt, Afterwords* Collection, Autumn/Winter 2002, Designer: Hussein Chalayan, Musee d'Art Moderne Grand-Duc Jean, Luxembourg, Ane Christensen, *Citrus Bowl,* 1998, *Shredded Bowl,* 1999, Both designer: Ane Christensen, Both courtesy of Ane Christensen, Cor Unum, *Fragile,* Designer: Ben van Berkel, *Tommy,* Designer: Lars Spuybroek, DQ, *Carving Set,* Designer: Daniel Cusick, *Fusion Flatware,* Designer: Daniel Cusick, *Spoon Holder,* Designer: Daniel Cusick, Courtesy of DQ,

Eisenman Architects, Competition Entry for Church of the Year 2000, Rome, presentation model, 1996, Designer: Peter Eisenman, Collection Centre Canadien d'Architecture/ Canadian Centre for Architecture, Montréal, Peter Eisenman Archive, Gehry Partners, Times Square model, 1998, Designer: Frank Gehry, Courtesy of Gehry Partners, Harmon/Kardon, *iSub, SoundSticks,* Both courtesy of Harmon/Kardon, Hold Everything, Black pencils, Kartell, *Portariviste,* Designer: Giotto Stoppino, Courtesy of Kartell, Leonardo, *Swing Glasses,* Lockheed Martin Aeronautics Company, Stealth Fighter Model, Designer: David Hudson, DC Models, Luminair, Inc., *Neon Night Light,* Courtesy of Luminair, Inc., Ingo Maurer, *Porca Miseria* lamp, Designer: Ingo Maurer, The Museum of Modern Art, New York, Miyake Design Studio, *Colombe,* Designer: Issey Miyake, Courtesy of Miyake Design Studio, Mono Tabletop, *Filio* fruit tray, Designer: Ralph Krämer, Courtesy of Mono Tabletop, Giovanni Pagnotta, *424.01,* 2001, Designer: Giovanni Pagnotta, Courtesy of Giovanni Pagnotta, Salter Housewares, *Bathroom Scales-9985 Digital Glass Scales,* Courtesy of Salter Housewares, Schimmel Pianos, *Pegasus Grand CC 208 P,* Designer: Luigi Colani, Vitry, Cuticle pushers, Tweezers, Malte Wagenfeld, *Ceiling Fan Type 1,* Designer: Malte Wagenfeld, Courtesy of Malte Wagenfeld, xO, *POAA,* 1999, Designer: Philippe Starck, Courtesy of xO   GALLERY D: *Design Afoot: Athletic Shoes, 1995–2000,* Organized by the San Francisco Museum of Modern Art, Hussein Chalayan, Selected works from the *Medea, 1866, 612 X 456 mm, oil on canvas, AF Sandys* Collection, Spring/Summer 2002 collection, Made possible in part by the Wexner Center Residency Award program
          GALLERY E: Sachiko Kodama and Minako Takeno, *Protrude, Flow,* 2001, Mixed media, Courtesy of Sachiko Kodama and Minako Takeno, Fabian Marcaccio, *Paint-Ball Robot,* 2001, Mixed media, Courtesy of Fabian Marcaccio, SIMPARCH, *Free Basin,* Birch wood, metal supports, Courtesy of SIMPARCH, A project by SIMPARCH in collaboration with Peter Eng, Pat Finlay, Chris Vorhees, and Hamza Walker. Organized for the Hyde Park Art Center of Chicago by Lia Alexopoulos and sponsored by Mesa Development Corporation, Alien Workshop: Various skateboards, Courtesy of DNA Distribution, BMW, BMW *Street Carver,* Courtesy of BMW of North America, Bontrager, *Race X-Lite Carbon Road, Race X-Lite Road,* Both courtesy of Trek Bicycles, Burton Snowboards, Various snowboards, Courtesy of Burton Snowboards, Cannondale Corporation, *Jekyll 700 Feminine, MT Tandem* bike, *Multisport 700 si, Scalpel, Super Silk,* All

courtesy of BikeSource and Cannondale Corporation, Deca, Various skateboards, Courtesy of Dwindle Distribution, Enjoi, Various skateboards, Courtesy of Dwindle Distribution, FibreFlex, *Leemo Kicktail 38"*, *Leemo Pro 36"*, *Pintail 44"*, *Response Slalom 27.875"*, Courtesy of FibreFlex, Firm, Various skateboards, Courtesy of BLITZ Distribution, Flex-Dex, Various skateboards, Courtesy of Flex-Dex, Flip, Various skateboards, Courtesy of BLITZ Distribution, Flowlab LLC, *Flowlab 32"*, 36", 42", Courtesy of Flowlab LLC, Foundation Skateboards, Various skateboards, Courtesy of Tumyeto Distribution, Gaastra, *Gaastra 4.0*, Courtesy of Chris Neville, Gary Fisher Bicycles Inc., *02 Sugar 1*, *02 Sugar 2+ Disk*, *02 SuperCal* 29" bike, Courtesy of Gary Fisher Bicycles, Inc., Giant Bikes, *Cypress DS, Prodigy DX, Prodigy DX* cast aluminum wheels, All courtesy of BikeSource and Giant Bikes, GNU, *Alter Gen, Carbon High Beam, Temple Cummins 160*, All courtesy of Mike Portman, Gordon & Smith, *Classic Noserider, Magic Fish, Perfecto, Squash*, All courtesy of Gordon & Smith, GT, *Bestwick Pro*, Courtesy of Pacific Cycle, Hammacher Schlemmer, *Lee Iacoca Electric Mini-Bicycle, Overland Electric Tow Vehicle, The Powered Parachute*, All courtesy of Hammacher Schlemmer, Haro Bicycle Corporation, *Escape 8.2, Extreme X3, Mirra Pro, Monocoque USA, Revo Mag, SR 2.0*, 24", *SR 71, TR 2.0 Track and Trail, Werks DHR, Werks XCS*, All courtesy of Haro Bicycle Corporation, Hoffman Bikes, *Condor, EP*, Both courtesy of Hoffman Bikes, Hollywood, Various skateboards, Courtesy of Tumyeto Corporation, Hook-Ups, Various skateboards, Courtesy of BLITZ Distribution, Huffy Bicycles, *Half Ton, M80, One Ton, Quarter Ton, Star 69, Super Deluxe, TL–88*, All courtesy of Huffy Bicycles, Klein Bicycles, *02 Carribean Reef Attitude, 02 USPS Masters Quantum Pro*, Both courtesy of Klein Bicycles, K2, Various in-line skates, Courtesy of Galyan's, Various snow skis, Courtesy of Galyan's, LeMond Bicycles, *Custom Program 02 "Blue Script", Custom Program 02 "Blue Sun"*, Both courtesy of LeMond Bicycles, Lib Technologies, *Lib Tech Matt Cummins 159, Lib Tech TRS series 162*, Both courtesy of Mike Portman, Line, Various snow blades, Courtesy of Galyan's, Macho Products, Inc., *Redman Self Defense Instructor Suit*, 1999, Courtesy of Macho Products, Inc., Mongoose, *SGX* racing frame, Courtesy of Pacific Cycle, Never Summer, Various snowboards, Courtesy of Never Summer, Perception, Inc., *Corona, Five-O, Jib, Lucid, Shadow, Shock, Sonic*, All courtesy of Perception, Inc., Pig, Various skateboards, Courtesy of Tumyeto Corporation, Real Skateboards, Various skateboards, Courtesy of Deluxe SF Distribution, Redline, *RL 360, Signature Team, Supa X*, All courtesy of Westerville Bike, Rossignol, Various snow skis, Courtesy of Galyan's, Sailworks, R+D Loft, *Revolution 7*, Designer: Bruce Peterson, Courtesy of Sailworks, R+D Loft, *Sailworks 5.6* and *Sailworks 7.5*, Courtesy of Chris Neville, Salomon, *Buzz 90* snow blade, *Teneighty Mogul* snow skis, Various in-line skate frames, *Verse 7* snow skis, All courtesy of Galyan's, Schwinn, *Andrew Faris "Azrael"*, Courtesy of Pacific Cycle, Sector 9, Various skateboards, Courtesy of Sector 9, Slingshot, *B-2, Torque*, Both courtesy of Mike Portman, Toy Machine, Various skateboards, Courtesy of Tumyeto Corporation, Trek Bicycles, High performance saddles, Mountain bar and stem combo, Road bar and stem combo, *02 Diesel DH, 02 5900 USPS, 02 Fuel Secret Service Bike, 02 "Project One" Pave Flambe, 02 "Project One" Saberline, 02 STP 400, 02 USPS Team Time Trial*, All courtesy of Trek Bicycles, Turner Downhill, Various skateboards, Courtesy of Bob Turner, Wills Wing, *Talon*, Courtesy of Wills Wing.

As an architect, I love each of my buildings as if it were my child, and likewise, as I look back on them, I love each of my MOMA exhibitions. Yet, I must confess to secretly harboring a special affection for *Machine Art,* my 1934 survey of the expression of the ideals of modernism in the products of industrial design. The pundits loathed it, the public loved it, and nowadays historians side with me—my favorite ending! More than any other design exhibition before or since, *Machine Art* put the idea of Art in the foreground, in the very title itself. It declared in no uncertain terms that of all of the exhibition's themes, from the revolutionary effects of manufacturing to the triumph of form and function to the manifestation of a zeitgeist, the most important was the question of aesthetics. In the years since, I have one by one set aside the tenets of modernism, yet I have never wavered in my conviction that the job of every architect and every designer is to give the world more art, more new, beautiful, and fascinating things to see.

Thus I was delighted when Jeffrey Kipnis and Annetta Massie told me of their plan to revisit the *Machine Art* show in their Wexner Center exhibition, *Mood River.* But when I reviewed their proposal, was I befuddled! *Mood River* seemed at first to have no connection to *Machine Art* at all. Where *Machine Art* sought timeless beauty in the spare precision of the modern, *Mood River* revels in excess, in the flamboyant forms and wild colors that are the stuff of fad and fashion. Yet, reminded of the duet Nietzsche choreographed between Apollo and Dionysus, I began to grasp a strange kinship between the two exhibitions.

I will leave it to others to decide whether or not Mr. Kipnis's speculative conjectures about the *Mood River* flow diagram hold any water. I doubt they do, even if they are damn fun to read. It does not matter anyway, who cares if he's right or wrong, I could gaze at that mesmerizing flow diagram all day—I might even turn it into a building! And I love his notion that new forms in art and design and even new ideas are all really just new feelings in the world. New ideas I take for granted, but new feelings? Delicious!

But I embrace Ms. Massie's bittersweet motto, "between yesterday and tomorrow is today," the *sine qua non* of the exhibition. Indeed, between the past and the future is Today, the fleeting present, and though we fight with all our heart to hold onto it forever, Today never lasts very long at all. *Mood River* celebrates the great lesson Heraclitus first taught three thousand years ago, that the only unchanging truth in the world is that everything changes. When the *Machine Art* catalogue was reprinted in celebration of its sixtieth anniversary, I wrote in its new foreword, "How much has changed! Chaos theory has replaced classical certainties. We prefer Heraclitian flux to Platonic Ideas, the principle of uncertainty to the model of perfection, complexity to simplicity." I might as well have been writing the proposal for *Mood River.*

As much as I am flattered by the curators' fascination with *Machine Art,* I am even more thrilled by their decision to stray from it. I am enchanted, for example, at the addition of clothing design to the mix through the work of the incomparable Issey Miyake, and the marvelous young upstart, Hussein Chalayan. Where else does functional design so affect our everyday life as an artistic practice? But most of all I delight in the inclusion of painting, sculpture, and architecture. Where *Machine Art* steered clear of fine art in favor of the utilitarian and machine-made as a matter of principle, *Mood River* brazenly extends its survey of sensibilities beyond design to consider work by some of our greatest contemporary artists and some of our most promising young artists. In 1934, the foreword to *Machine Art* stated, "Good machine art is entirely independent of painting, sculpture and architecture." It was as foolish a statement then as it is today, of course. Though fine art is very different from design, nevertheless they each influence one another, a point this exhibition makes and with poignant impact.

As I ponder the fate that befell the Less is More philosophy that governed *Machine Art,* I recall a scene in Hamlet, where Gertrude chides Iago, "More Matter, less Art," a remark that might have as easily been made by Mies. I think this exhibition teaches us a better lesson: More Matter, More Art!

PHILIP JOHNSON
NEW CANAAN, AUGUST 2001

It is in part through the aesthetic appreciation of natural forms that man has carried on his spiritual conquest of nature's hostile chaos. Today man is lost in the far more treacherous wilderness of industrial and commercial civilization. On every hand machines literally multiply our difficulties and point our doom. If, to use L. P. Jack's phrase, we are to "end the divorce between our industry and our culture we must assimilate the machine aesthetically as well as economically." Not only must we bind Frankenstein—but we must make him beautiful.

Would that those words were mine, but in fact they belong to the redoubtable Alfred H. Barr, Jr., founding director and messianic visionary behind the Museum of Modern Art who, sixty-eight years ago, concluded his foreword to the *Machine Art* catalogue with that eerily prescient paragraph. As Wexner Center curators Jeffrey Kipnis and Annetta Massie found their embarkation point for *Mood River* in Philip Johnson's seminal *Machine Art* exhibition of 1934, I relished the occasion to seek in Mr. Barr a bit of directorial inspiration and, as always, found it in more than ample measure. After all, it can be argued that Barr invented the very notion of a multidisciplinary museum, where art and design, high culture and low, could cohabitate and cast sly but lucid shadows upon each other. A place like the Wexner Center might never have emerged were it not for Barr's radical dream; our debt to him and his pioneering colleagues is incalculable.

Even so, *Mood River* is no mere reprise meant as fawning tribute to the masters. Rather, it is a spirited homage to the enduring vitality of their project, even through seven decades of swirling and sometimes contentious currents in cultural theory. Bravely conjoining art and design in their survey, Kipnis and Massie posit as their premise the startling coherence of creative flows, revealing and magnifying for us often surprising simultaneities across diverse practices and disciplines. Their ambition is no less than to bottle within the exhibition those fleeting effervescences and efflorescences that mark a moment and capture the very mood and feel of our time.

Their métier is the migration of evocative shapes, colors, and materials that course through the visual fabric of our lives. Nothing is too lofty or too lowly for their scrutiny: pens and pencils, shaving equipment, cutlery, medical devices, housewares and household implements, lighting, furniture, art, musical instruments, and sports equipment—all claiming every purpose under heaven from efficiency to efficacy to comfort to seduction to beauty. If the preponderance of lithe and voluptuous shapes in the *River* contrasts with the obdurate, articulated forms of the *Machine*, one need only remember the dizzying discoveries in

technology that allowed that evolution over seventy years. But common to both *Mood* and *Machine* is intense appreciation for the aesthetics of function and the function of aesthetics.

While some will exult in the sheer dazzle of the *River*'s display, others will find in its very sparkle cause for skepticism if not outright hostility. Therein lies the curatorial peril of such a foray, especially at a time of critical backlash against so many allegedly undisciplined exhibitions of popular culture. But *Mood River* stands as an act of bold conviction, embedded as it is in the historic, scientific, philosophical, and emotional context that Kipnis so deftly conjures while Massie tends to the exquisite intricacies of the objects themselves. With their ingenious installation designer, José Oubrerie, they have taken us through eddies and rapids and bends in the *River* that we might never have navigated on our own. In some places, they have mapped new waters entirely, and have invited us to join in the pleasure and serendipity of their discoveries. Whether or not one trusts their curatorial cartography, the exuberance of its territorial ambition is undeniable. *Mood River* celebrates the very phenomenon of fluidity as it traces the impulses, ideas, and expressions that measure the water table of contemporary life.

Even casual immersion in *Mood River* reveals the enormity of the undertaking (or should I say undertow?). We are grateful to the numerous artists, designers, and lenders who have shared their treasures with us. As always, we are pleased to recognize the many dedicated members of the extended exhibition team. To Chief Exhibition Designer James A. Scott and his crew of designers and installers, we express our utmost respect and appreciation for braving the rapids with such expertise. To Registrar Joan Hendricks and her team, we extend more than a thousand thanks for their heroic handling of the more than a thousand objects in the show. Curatorial assistants and graduate associates Amy Schmersal, Joby Pottmeyer, and Rujuta Mody brought near military precision to the enterprise under the watchful gaze of Exhibitions Manager Jill Davis, our trusty field marshal for the department.

Director of Administration Gretchen Metzelaars, Director of Marketing and Communications Darnell Lautt, Public Relations Manager Karen Simonian, and Marketing Manager Liz Alcalde all brought crucial energy and enthusiasm to this unwieldy endeavor. Former Director of Development Beth Fisher and Grants Manager Jeff Byars transformed paper proposals into real resources, leading the way to a splendid array of sponsors. And Director of Education Patricia Trumps gathered a stellar cast of cultural commentators, designers, and performers to punctuate the exhibition throughout its run. We welcome the partnership of Rob Livesey, Director of Ohio State University's Knowlton School of Architecture, in presenting these programs.

This publication reflects the boundless dedication and meticulous attention of Editor Ann Bremner, who has presided over a brilliant roster of essayists. We are indebted to Sanford Kwinter, Chee Pearlman, Sylvia Lavin, and José Oubrerie for their vibrant and illuminating texts, as we are to Philip Johnson for his benevolent "benediction." Designer Patrick Li of Work in Progress infused the catalogue and exhibition graphics with just the right viscosity in an elegant arabesque. Our Senior Graphic Designer, Jeff Packard, honored the spirit of that design in all manner of related materials.

And now, a few words *for* our sponsor... a familiar refrain that may once have invited instant distraction now reworked to request your ardent attention. Battelle deserves no less for its magnificent generosity as *Mood River*'s exclusive lead sponsor. Former President and CEO Doug Oleson and new President and CEO Carl Kohrt have our thanks for their visionary leadership in this collaboration. We are enormously gratified by the support of Ben Maiden, Senior Vice President, Chemical Products; Rich Rosen, Senior Vice President, Pharmaceutical and Medical Products; and Larry Barbera, Director, Industrial Design, Pharmaceutical and Medical Products, all of whom recognized the affinities between the exhibition and Battelle's own focus on creative innovation. In addition, we appreciate the sincere efforts of Jerry Bahlmann, Senior Vice President for Administration and General Counsel; Karen Hollern, Director, Community Relations; and Tom McClain, Vice President, Corporate Communications, in bringing this partnership to fruition.

We also express our heartfelt gratitude to Peter Lewis, whose generous commitment to pioneering practices in art and design has propelled his connection to preeminent cultural and educational institutions nationwide, and the Wexner Center is proud to now be among them. Agnes Gund and Daniel Shapiro responded with customary enthusiasm and amplitude to *Mood River*, and it is always an honor to recognize their exceptional cultural patronage. Major support is also provided by Accenture and Shiseido Co., Ltd. to whom we are most grateful. The National Endowment for the Arts, the Ohio Arts Council, The Ohio State University Division of Student Affairs, Coca-Cola, and the Corporate Annual Fund of the Wexner Center Foundation have also contributed to the realization of *Mood River*, and WBNS 10 TV has provided promotional support.

Exhibitions of this magnitude are unthinkable without the moral and financial support of trustees, and the Wexner Center is blessed by board members who embrace the mission of this institution with heart, mind, and soul. They are incomparable.

Mood River is, of course, a playful nod to Henry Mancini's theme for *Breakfast at Tiffany's*. With that in mind, I'd like to close with a bit of lyrical license. Kipnis and Massie, two drifters off to see the world, certainly crossed the *River* in style. We're glad they found their rainbow's end at the Wexner Center.

SHERRI GELDIN
DIRECTOR, WEXNER CENTER FOR THE ARTS

Battelle is very proud to be the lead sponsor of the Wexner Center for the Arts' *Mood River* exhibition.

The message conveyed through *Mood River* strongly supports Battelle's objective of educating a global community, young and old, about the value of combining art and science viewpoints to achieve new innovations.

As a global organization whose mission ranges from new product design and development to advanced materials to improved primary and secondary education, Battelle is pleased this exhibition is being held in greater Columbus. With our motto being "The Business of Innovation," we welcome this strong alliance with the highly innovative minds of the Wexner Center for the Arts and the curators of the *Mood River* exhibition.

CARL F. KOHRT
PRESIDENT AND CEO
BATTELLE

Between yesterday and tomorrow is today, a time of unprecedented production and consumption of objects that simultaneously create and fulfill specific attractions, moods, and desires. *Mood River* explores the unexpected connections among a myriad of such objects—things as diverse as a jump rope, a wristwatch, a cigarette lighter, an ink pen, and a salt shaker—and investigates how these connections in color, form, and materials even flow into more rarified works of art.

As curators, Jeffrey Kipnis and I were primed for adventurous forays. We spent time in galleries and museums but even more time devouring popular magazines, going on lengthy shopping sprees, and attending international trade fairs and conventions. We learned commercial shoptalk and relied on marketers for introductions and information as we went in search of the essential ingredients that make the newest products and materials so alluring if not downright indispensable. We withdrew from subjective opinions regarding usefulness and uselessness and focused on form, light, color, technology, and innovation to see how our material world aligns itself at this distinct moment. We were horrified at some findings, eternally grateful for others; we found things necessary to sustain even save lives, amid things that simply make us happy and comfortable, things we cannot live with and things we cannot live without.

In mass-produced and mass-marketed objects we witnessed the interplay of perpetually morphing forms and continuously developing substances and processes. We marveled at how new technologies produce constant innovation. And we discovered those forms, materials, textures, and colors that, through repetition and familiarity, make today look and feel like today. We tracked forms we named voluptuous (curvaceous and sensual), stealth (fractal and jagged, from the Stealth Fighter), and minimal (reductive and stark)—and identified approaches to color we termed "five-flavor" (for the propensity to produce objects in a rainbow of hues, from the classic five flavors/colors of Life Savers) and "trans" (for the varieties of transparency and translucency—from crystalline to murky—we encountered with such frequency). We found these characteristics everywhere amid everything, and traced them also into the realm of art. In the orchestration of the exhibition as a whole, each characteristic creates a distinctive sound or tone that joins with others in chords and choruses.

We fortunately agreed about most things—both uncomfortable with anything figurative and relieved to find reductive or abstract approaches in which new forms and colors sing. We made up arbitrary rules to which we imperfectly adhered: we would have nothing to do with anything brown, living, or dead, and no wheels, balls, wood, or glass, among other criteria. We had misgivings about anything retro or nostalgic, though we admired objects in which tradi-

tional functions were recast in nontraditional shapes or materials. A perfect example is the extraordinary *Pegasus* piano designed by Luigi Colani for the Schimmel company. In it the natural and faux veneers of the past become entirely synthetic—more a sensual spaceship than a musical instrument—and it comes in any color of auto paint available.

We often felt lost in the surplus of stuff, overwhelmed by the fact we would never see everything. Our plans changed frequently along the way. We abandoned an early passion for pink and green and moved beyond an initial fascination with orchids and insects as models of forms in flux. And, of course, not every object or artwork we hoped to feature was available for the exhibition. We regret the absence of Saporiti's unforgettable Voyager Nest—a triumph of organic form and synthetic material—and of artworks by Ellsworth Kelly, among other examples. Happily, however, a lively team of curatorial assistants and colleagues facilitated the acquisition of many hundreds of items for the show. Months of research, phone calls, and missives led to almost daily deliveries of the most unusual packages. The mail room may never recover or have so much fun again. It was an unorthodox way of working—but the only way that worked.

Most people don't spend a lot of time thinking about either art or design: they respond to what they see, often in similarly subjective ways, despite the clear differences between the two broad disciplines. Designers seek to fulfill functional intentions (at least in theory) and achieve concrete results; artists are less concerned with practical functionality. A successful product design might result in a zillion exact replicas; artworks still tend to exist as unique objects or perhaps limited sets. Yet both art and design create objects that are emotionally and socially charged and involve complex webs of practical, aesthetic, political, and economic issues. Both challenge their own traditions, and, these days, both often rely on computer-generated techniques, multimedia formats, and hands-off fabrications. What interested us were the myriad ways contemporary art and design work with a shared vocabulary, with design emphasizing sensation along with function and artworks drawing on many of the same effects we saw in design objects.

For the exhibition, we envisioned an installation that immersed viewers in a river of art and design while keeping each distinct, floating separately though, as we hope to reveal, in common waters. We also sought to convey a fluid sequence of moods—which we captioned Bliss, Ecstasy, Trauma, and Rage—as visitors moved along the river. The opening gallery was conceived as a composition in which the gestures of design transform acute minimal precision into sheer sensuality, solid geometries into iridescence and mist, stark whiteness into bliss and serenity. The sculptures of Siobhán Hapaska share biomorphic concerns with the designs of Greg Lynn's shelving system and Elsa Peretti's *Bean.* An installation of lamps features lights that drip, inflate, knot, fold, shimmer, and glow. Tabletop objects, furniture, and fashions share unexpected relationships, between, for example, flat and folded in chairs by Polyline and origami sculptures by Enlai Hooi. Sarah Schwartz's *Perfect Veil,* the Transformables that change from rain coat to tent, and Servo's clear plastic furniture demonstrate a range of translucencies and transparencies.

In the second gallery, the suggested mood is ecstasy, and organic forms predominate. A school of fish composed of hundreds of sundries swims above a coral reef of taillights leading to a surging waterfall of furniture. Early in our research, we were amazed and captivated by the collision of personality and design at car shows (well-populated pageants of beauty, commerce, and lust). There, each year, new models debut: adjusted, "improved," and made different in some slight or grand manner from those of the year before. Rather than focus on automobile bodies, we honed in on the genre of taillights, indexical markers of change—if not progress. We found extremes of vigorous and exotic fixtures next to the most static, mundane, and even ugly appliqués of plastic, and we obsessively critiqued them all, photographed them, and spoke of their features and disappointments ad nauseam. Our friends became aware of our scrutiny, and even apologetic if their auto's lamps were not chosen for the exhibition.

The school of fish installation is a dense and swirling composition made from a multitude of hanging objects that are common, practical, and easy to obtain—things that take care of us, keep us company, and relieve stresses: toothbrushes and other grooming utensils, pens and power saws, cutlery, electronic gadgets, and many attractive things formerly unknown to us (though we found they belong to a kitchen, tool shed, or office). These personal devices satisfy required needs and acquired tastes by rejecting their former stylistic manifestation for ever more sophisticated, sleek, colorful, and appealing forms that woo consumers by so presciently responding to, or even creating, their moods.

The furniture waterfall reflects a similarly varied spectrum of attitudes and forms in chairs. Like most consumers, we were amateurs but quick studies, finding the most rewarding examples to be holistic and soothing, gentle on the eyes and emotions. Philippe Starck's *Bubble Collection* of furniture treats minimal forms with flair, creating pieces that are conceptually solid but physically thin-shelled and hard, their pastel insides vacuumed away. The resolutely reduced forms of Quinze & Milan vibrate with chromatic contrasts and intensities and juxtapose hard-edged Flintstone mass with surprising softness. The waterfall rises dramatically and then pours over the wall spanning two galleries to show pieces out of normal context: off the floor, at every angle, skewing views and expectations. Divorcing the chairs from any semblance of practical functionality and reveling in sheer form, the installation enables viewers to recognize unexpected visual links to objects throughout the exhibition.

The next gallery, the Wexner Center's largest, is intended to suggest the trauma of wholesale transformation. Here one finds the major works we called "whales," monumental beasts that move through the river with undeniable purpose, presence, and stature. Viewers can revel in the chromatic shapes of David Reed's painting and John Chamberlain's sculpture, the explosions of E. V. Day and Ingo Maurer, the voluptuousness of works by Issey Miyake, Frank Gehry, and Frank Stella, the transparency of Tony Cragg, and the strikingly inventive and deconstructive excess of Hussein Chalayan. In the same space the enduring forms of the Stealth Fighter (at ⅙ scale)

are as breathtaking and heart accelerating as any sculptural experience. Juxtaposed with the whales are the "sprites": tweezers, turbines, tumblers, computer apparatus, and a host of other objects that echo the whales' visual attributes.

The contrasts continue in an adjacent space, where (during the later weeks of the exhibition) we present a selection of designs from Chalayan's Spring 2002 collection, as well as Chee Pearlman's miniature "museum" of plastic cups. Chalayan's collection, which won significant critical acclaim when it debuted in Paris in October 2001, was commissioned by the Wexner Center and created with the support of a Wexner Center Residency Award for 2001–02. Pearlman's collection demonstrates the formal and material variations evident in even the simplest and most disposable things.

Dynamic and outrageous, the works in the final gallery express rage, but less in the sense of anger than of passion and intensity, qualities our culture often aligns with sports. We were fascinated by how sophisticated design and twenty-first-century materials have permeated every aspect of sports, even making possible the emergence of extreme sports. We became aficionados of 'boards, bikes, and blades, and we started watching the X games, visiting sports stores, reading sports publications. We envisioned the installation in this gallery taking the form of tornados of sports equipment: vortices of tents, sails, surfboards, skateboards, bicycles, and shoes, all swirling in space from high ceiling to floor.

In addition to these elements, we decided to feature an installation called *Free Basin*, an indoor and fully operational skateboard bowl by the architectural collaborative SIMPARCH, which visitors are welcome to use. As specialized research we took a road trip to Skatopia and its Museum of Skateboard History in rural southern Ohio, where we received a real-life introduction to the world of extreme sports and the acrobatics of skateboarding. We returned from another field trip with a sling shot and paintballs, then recalled that artist Fabian Marcaccio has created his own take on this sport with his *Paint-Ball Robot,* and gleefully added it to the exhibition. During *Mood River*'s later weeks it will take *Free Basin*'s place as the active pièce de résistance in this final gallery. The *Robot* slowly shoots colored balls one at a time with the seemingly mindless duplication of the most mundane factory production; over time, its mechanical regularity produces a computer-generated image.

Throughout our investigations we immersed ourselves in new things, discovering not only their commonalities but also how quickly newness fades. *Design Afoot: Athletic Shoes 1995–2000*, the "show within a show" that for the exhibition's first weeks serves as a preamble to the sports installations of the last gallery, clearly demonstrates the swift passage of design time, since many shoes that were prototypes or new introductions when *Design Afoot* premiered at the San Francisco Museum of Modern Art in July 2000 are now vintage. The development of new things often reflects (or prefigures) unconscious desires; choosing them allowed us to create a microcosm of this moment. We found a river that constantly regenerates as it flows from yesterday to tomorrow. Fortunately, retro never lasts. Perhaps even more fortunately, neither does the new. The reward of our search was simply seeing what is there now.

ANNETTA MASSIE is Associate Curator of Exhibitions at the Wexner Center. She has organized varied group exhibitions, as well as solo exhibitions and projects by artists including Ernesto Neto, Beverly Semmes, Udomsak Krisanamis, and Rirkrit Tiravanija.

left to right
BREZZA SOSPENSIONE
Designer: Andrea Anastasio
Courtesy of/photo courtesy of Artemide

LIQUID_LIGHT DROP_4, 2000
Designer: Hopf + Wortmann
LIQUID_LIGHT DROP_ceiling, 2000
Designer: Hopf + Wortmann
LIQUID_LIGHT DROP_3, 2000
Designer: Hopf + Wortmann
Courtesy of/photos courtesy of
Hopf + Wortmann, Munich

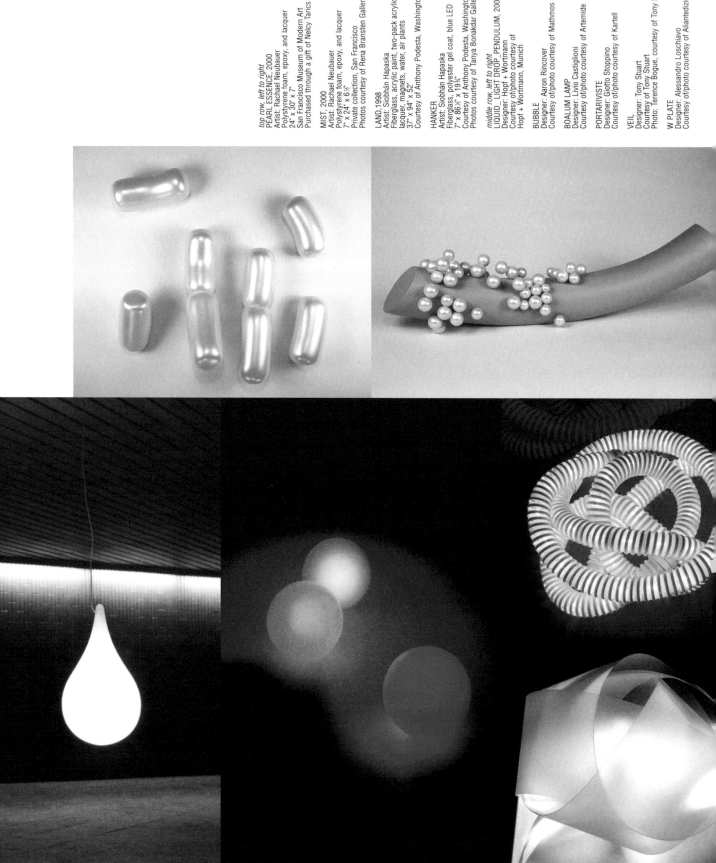

bottom row, left to right:
KNOT LAMP
Designer: Janos Korban, Stefanie Flaubert
Courtesy Korban/Flaubert

PERFECT VEIL
Designer: Sarah Schwartz
Courtesy of Sarah Schwartz
Photo: Roman Sapecki

FOLDING
Paper
Artist: Enlai Hooi
Courtesy of Enlai Hooi

FOLDER CHAIR
Designer: Stephan Schöning
Courtesy of Polyline

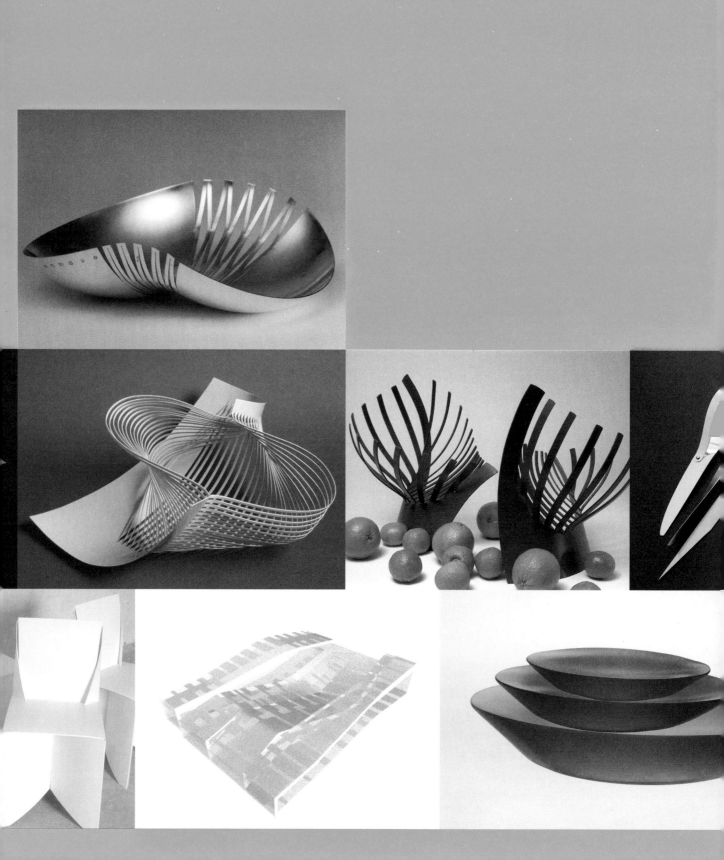

top
CRACKED BOWL, 2000
Designer: Ane Christensen
Courtesy of Ane Christensen
Photo: Dominic Sweeney

middle row, left to right
SHREDDED BOWL, 1999
Designer: Ane Christensen
CITRUS BOWL, 1998
Designer: Ane Christensen
Courtesy of Ane Christensen
Photos: Dominic Sweeney

LETTER OPENERS
Designers: various
BENBECULA, 1961
Designer: Enzo Mari
Courtesy of/photos courtesy of Danese Milano

bottom row, left to right
FOLDER CHAIR
Designer: Stephan Schöning
Courtesy of Polyline
Photo courtesy of Stephan Schöning, Polyline

THERMO-CLINE
Courtesy of/photo courtesy of Servo

ANTIPODI, 1990
Danese Milano
Designer: Marco Ferreri
Courtesy of/photo courtesy of Danese Milano
(two views)

BEAN MINAUDIÈRE, 1974
Designer: Elsa Peretti for Tiffany & Co.
Courtesy of Tiffany & Co., New York
Photo: Josh Haskins, courtesy of Tiffany & Co.

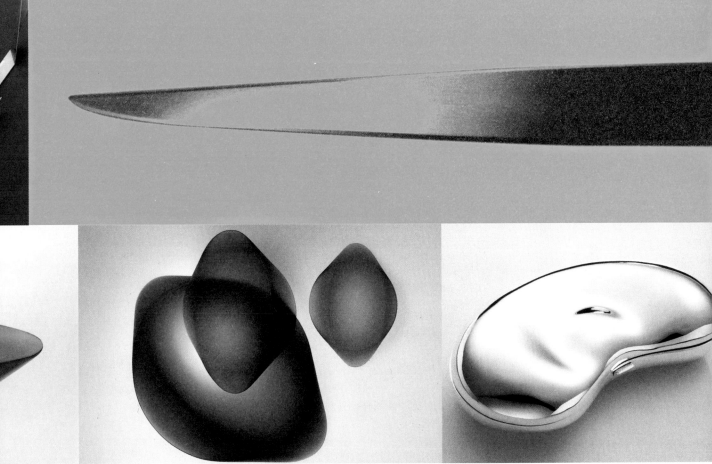

ENRON WIND TURBINE BLADE
Courtesy of the City of Storm Lake, Iowa, and the
Storm Lake Chamber of Commerce
Photo courtesy of Enron Wind

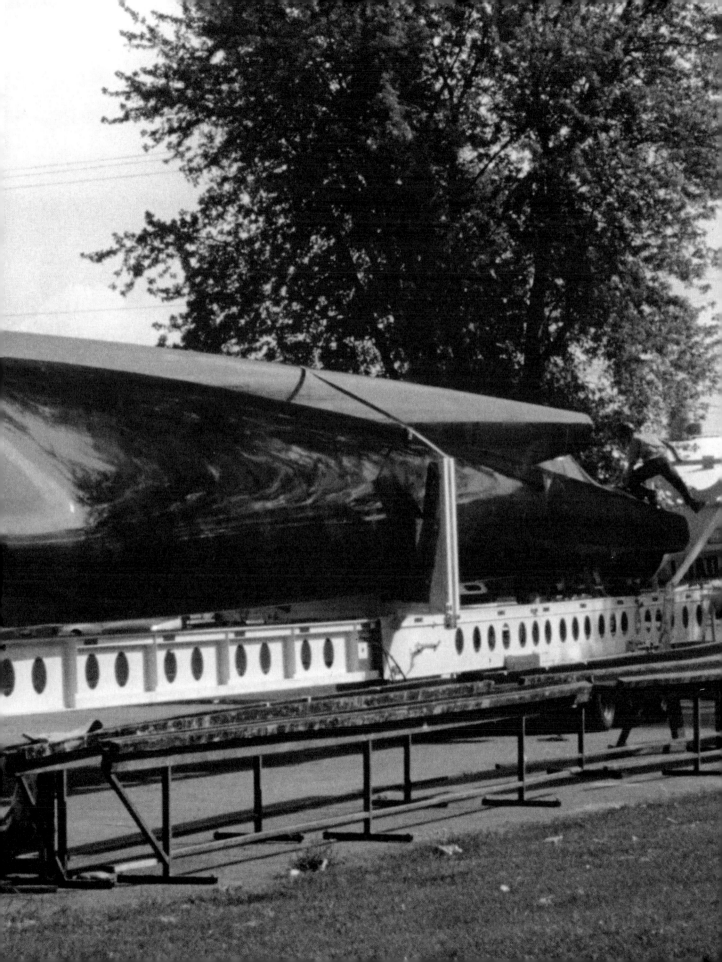

Mood River is a study of invisibilities and of invisible coherence. It is made possible by nothing else than a nervous system so exotic and refined that it can deduce movement and regularity where none has measurably occurred. That nervous system is of course the human one—our own—and a marvel of the design process itself. It is the necessary invention of a universe that needed to shorten its own product runs, a universe that needed a better, quicker, and more nuanced means to sense itself. *Mood River* is thus not only about sensing, but about sensation itself, and more than anything about sensibility. Let none of these words take a back seat to concepts ever again.

Around 1990, something discernable began to emerge in the world of advanced design. A maritime, hydraulic, or rheological theme began to be heard, softly, remotely yet everywhere behind the appearances of things. The world of things began increasingly to manifest its kinship with the spontaneous and cybernetic design processes of nature, necessarily calling forth an espousal of life and of the creative wages of time. Transitions and behaviors were becoming the new objects of formal attention, the new focuses of research in form. One could have called it design's first Copernican revolution (design never underwent a modernist revolution like that of music, painting, or science) but in many ways it was the opposite of that. It was a new animism, a descent into the primary materiality of the premodern cosmos. It was the early stirring of *Mood River*.

Despite their celebrated storms and ecstasies the Ancients did not yet refer to moods, but to *movements of the soul*. Later Medievals pictured an internal landscape of striving *humors*—literal fluids in struggle for ascendancy and richly endowed with qualities like slowness, brittleness, ropiness, or solvency. Every mixture was thought to produce novel atmospheres, attitudes, and sensations. Today we partly and secretly envy—even as we publicly dismiss— our ancestors' purer, turbulent, and childlike worlds. Feeling obliged by our "enlightenment," we had no choice but to choose universal laws and essences over the unbearable and perpetual corruptions of time. For the Ancients, however, everything—all of life—could be found in the *turning (tropein)*, in the transition from *this* to *that*. We, of course, continue to seek what we think of as a deeper meaning in what remains at rest.

But we all know that life is more than just a series of successful consolidations. Yet does life stream through us, or do we move through *it*? Either way, in life, one thing always moves against another, and every actor and worldly component is changed through these messy and restless encounters. In other words, not only do we change, but our world does as well; for when something novel appears in the world, is it not the very sign and warranty of our own freedom to become? Life is a river and we are a school of fish.

Did I say we were like fish? I surely did not mean this, because, more truly, our resemblance is to that magical formation: the *school*. But to what matrix does a school pay homage? Out of which continuum does the organized twitching, the plastic geometries of the piscine field emerge? To that transparent, infinitely mysterious field of vectors, that marvel among things, to Water. *Vectors, vectors everywhere but not an object in sight....*

Water, the primordial fluid. A fluid is a confederacy of separate actors doomed to coherence because of their capacity to adhere. Where one atom of the stuff goes its neighbor follows—albeit more or less. This is the mandate of hydraulics: suction, coordination, flow. Yet all is not perfect harmony and alignment. Nothing is simple about fluids. Every difference in an hydraulic field gets registered, collected, remembered, and passed on; and once the ledger of this moving memory reaches the critical point, a new arabesque is reliably born. We call this new born thing a vortex. The vortex is what we worship in nature, it is the thing we call beauty, the source of everything violent and serene. The vortex is us.

Schools are vortexes made visible. Schools and vortexes are dynamic locales where information is created and distributed, where ambient intelligence is made incarnate, specific, historical. Vortexes are the expression of shaping forces collected and channeled from the outside and impressed on matter. To be impressed is nothing less than to be a vortex renewed. Matter itself is hidebound vortex, one whose forces have been subdued and confined. Fish are vortexes that have been stabilized; water, the field of unconstrained vortical possibility. Schools are the historical and behavioral incarnation of the encounter between the two. They are the places where freedom (or subjection) is *lived*.

Design has always been most vital and historical precisely where its vortical nature can be apprehended. But the vortex belongs to no one, it is what, in life, *we seek to capture,* not exactly to hold, but to let pass through us. One fish draws water through its gills to free the oxygen trapped there by climactic and geologic action, while another, like certain sharks, must drive its gills through water in order not to die. These swimmer-organisms long ago became specific vortex-objects to capture what other vortexes had previously deposited in the matter-world.

Even the pulsating whip of the tail of a swimming fish generates vortexes on either side of the animal, depositing pools of energy that the animal shamelessly taps to propel itself still further. Fish are so profoundly creatures of the vortex that they can achieve greater than 100 percent locomotor efficiency by reaping magically exactly what they sow.[1] Fish that hunt efficiently in darkness do so by tracking wakes, following the vortical trails of other swimmer-organisms, trails that can mark in a wake the invisible structure of water for more than fifty-five body lengths.[2] And at the end of each of these gossamer vortical strands, dinner moves in its own consolidated vortical form.

To locomote, to eat, to look and see, are each and equally activities of social and erotic predation. To live and to create is to hunt. Vortexes actually track other vortexes by virtue of their hydraulic nature, and as vortexes they can do no else. When we eat, we eat a portion of our world, a portion that when metabolized, becomes us. When we look, we equally strive to become our world, and when we see, we are struck for an instant by the fact that the world has momentarily become us. Our education trains us to believe that we recognize and eat objects, but at the heart of every act of aesthetic recognition, we know that what is happening is that one vortex is capturing, is being incorporated by, *is harmonizing with* another.

In time, the world could do no otherwise but to evolve beyond the phase where only animals were predacious, where only animals were capable of the variable tensions that constitute the humors and moods and movements of the soul. The hunt is largely a musical act, *the act of subduing and assimilating the vortical power of another being to that of oneself.* Today, we know that it is not only humans and animals that take part in this process, for our material world is now as deeply part of this broad musical ecology as any biological thing. The tunes of the manufactured world travel and diversify, collude and break away, just as birdsongs move through a forest population to establish kinship, territorial, and even martial relationships. Only now, in the technological world, the songs are presented to the eye, and through the eye they do their work to quicken or moderate the soul.

It would go too far to suggest that objects—especially the tawdry trinkets of our contemporary world—might possess souls with the capacity to be moved. We, on the other hand, surely have been guilty for two-and-a-half millennia of misattributing our own souls to something other than our material compositions. Our moods are internal weather, transitory inhabitations that damage and repair previous formations. They represent nothing more than creative disturbances in our physical organization. Mood is a disruption of the stasis of the soul, an interruption of its natural torpor, its tendency to repose. Mood is always production and disequilibrium, a setting of the world into motion, the connection of a quiescent vortex to a new and unknown one.

All movement in its origin is a passage toward both freedom and the unknown—toward the unexpected—even if it may sometimes seem that all movement ends badly. The evidence in our manufactured environment today rarely does more than hypostatize movement in plastic, represent it, reduce it to a crude indexical marking and to a digital-age version of the streamlining that supplied popular amusement in the early mid-century.

What is critical, and powerfully out of step with today's physical and intellectual commonplaces, is to grasp "the great river of time" that caught the imagination and instincts of the early century biologists and philosophers, the *symphony* of shaping forces that equally characterizes nature and the social and technical world. Henri Bergson described an *élan vital,* a universal force that drives living things continually out of phase with themselves in order that they may perpetually discover new configurations and new engagements with a necessarily moving reality. Conrad Waddington, the twentieth century's preeminent theoretical biologist, gave us the *chreod,* a term he coined from the Greek words for "necessary" and "route," because he too saw that the universe of matter was constrained absolutely by an overriding fact: that it not only followed a regulated *path,* but that it did so necessarily. Chreods represent the guides and directors, the invisible moving molds, in which the shapes of our world develop and whose imprint they bear. We never see the chreod directly but only in retrospect or as a kinship discernable within a mass.

What teaches us best today that matter is active, that the universe never sits still, that the distinction between the living and the inert, the born and the made, is neither where nor what we once thought it was? Not the industrial objects of the exhibition, at least not these per se. While their aesthetics celebrate a new fluidity springing from the alchemies of numerically driven manufacturing and design, they are but specters of the broader mega-vortexes of which they are a part, the larger, mysterious integrations that one can only call a new type of nature. The school of fish is certainly us, but it is also the material world itself in its startling, coherent integrality, the world that cannot help but flow together like lines in a fugue, the world in which vortexes migrate among the currents like rumors, refrains, viruses, weeds, and songs.

The once common word *Geist* is now, by broad consensus, out of date. We no longer accept the woolly and psychologizing "anthropomorphism" of a historical *Spirit,* but we like to muse scientifically and philosophically about *Zusammenhang* (the way things hang together), without suspecting how much each of these terms may ultimately rely on the other. The connecting tissue, like some ancient ether, owes everything to communication, to the loops and meshes and membranes across which information ceaselessly moves from one place in the universe to another.

Ours is a world fraught with technical relations, calculations, rationalities of every kind. The new look of things is not so much what is at stake in *Mood River* as the vibratory mesh that binds all of being together, the continuum of resonance that makes every moment, despite its apparent discontinuities, whole. The manufactured thing is rightly seen as a product of tools, and a reality saturated by tools, but the directorial lines that guide these things through the world are products of a living order larger than meets the eye.

To see the grand movements, the ensembles, is not only a form of communion with the world, it is, as Goethe might have said, a form of love.

The River has many states, and to each state corresponds a Mood: Bliss is the diffuse affect, the cloud, the tolerant love; Ecstasy, a nervous fulguration, a cascade born of terror and awe, a self-sufficient love; Rage, a storm of passion, a turbulence that seeks only discharge, reconciliation, and forgiveness; and Trauma, the love that leaves an indelible mark. These are the movements that remind us that looking at our world is limited if left to the metaphysics of eyes alone.

Writer, theorist, and editor, Sanford Kwinter is cofounder of ZONE publications and teaches at Rice University's School of Architecture. He is most recently author of Architectures of Time *(MIT).*

[1] Michael S. Triantafyllou and George S. Triantafyllou, "An Efficient Swimming Machine," *Scientific American* vol. 272, no. 3 (March 1995): 64–70.
[2] Kirsten Pohlmann, Frank W. Grasso, and Thomas Breithaupt, "Tracking Wakes: The Nocturnal Predatory Strategy of Piscivorous Catfish," *Proceedings of the National Academy of Sciences* vol. 98, no. 13 (online version, June 5, 2001), reported in *Science News,* vol. 159 (June 9, 2001). It is suspected that insects—animals that move through fluid air—possess these same vortex-reading habits.

JEFFREY KIPNIS

On those who step into the same river, different and still different waters flow
—Heraclitus of Ephesus

ON ITS SURFACE, MOOD RIVER OFFERS A REFLECTION on the characteristic shapes, materials, colors, textures, and luminosities that weave together to form the complex visual fabric of our lives. The exhibition scans the worlds of contemporary design and art to detect emerging threads of sensibility that titillate our senses; create the ambiences and atmospheres of our homes, shops, and offices; modulate our moods; pique our desires; and above all, make today feel like today.

Pick up any general interest magazine from 1992 and thumb through its incidental survey of the world, its collage of furniture, fashions, hairstyles, objects, advertisements, buildings, and works of art. Struck by how different the world looked only a decade ago, you notice something eerie, that it looked in retrospect strangely coordinated: its diverse elements of material life flow together in a palpable synchrony. It is not that one thing matched another in shape or color, but rather something more mysterious, as if exotic rhythms and harmonies that could not quite be grasped at the time were all along gathering the discordant cacophony of everyday life into a sublime symphony.

For centuries, experts and laypersons alike thought of this concordance as the effect of a great organizing force, the Zeitgeist, the Spirit of the Times. In recent years, the naïve notion of such a single spirit has given way to more subtle analyses. By tracing the interlacing of economy, social structure, science, technology, and signification, we are slowly coming to grasp our world as a multiplicity of emerging sensibilities, of spirits short-lived and long, that link at any given moment into a vast sea.

A Gentle Burlesque

Staged as a gentle burlesque on Philip Johnson's 1934 *Machine Art* exhibition at the Museum of Modern Art, *Mood River* draws hope from Karl Marx's wisecrack that world-historical events occur twice, first as Tragedy then as Farce. Contesting every premise of its forerunner, *Mood River* splashes over the containments Johnson so carefully erected nearly seventy years ago, spilling into gesture, color, and ornament, into fashion, even into art. Yet, despite the sharp differences in personality, appearance, and manners, the two are twins; upbringing is everything.

Before embarking on his legendary career as an architect, Philip Johnson founded the Department of Architecture and Design in Alfred Barr's newly formed New York Museum of Modern Art. Barr, a passionate advocate of the European avant-garde art and design movements, intended to use his new museum as a platform from which to bring up to date the matériel of contemporary life in the United States across its entire spectrum, from the lowest implement of daily use to the highest works of art, from house to city. Barr conceived the architecture and design program, recruiting Johnson as its minister. The brash young curator first introduced Modern

MUSEUM OF MODERN ART
MACHINE ART

Architecture to the U.S. audience in his seminal 1932 exhibition *International Style*, then turned to industrial production for his next curatorial contribution to his mentor's mission.

While perhaps not quite the Tragedy suggested by Marx—except in the opinion of Royal Cortissoz, New York *Herald Tribune* art critic at the time—*Machine Art* was, nevertheless, a sober, high-minded affair. Johnson assembled hundreds of products of modern industrial design, from housewares to furniture to machine parts to scientific instruments to exotica such as headlights and propellers, all evidencing the Bauhaus principles, ever so slightly mannered, that Johnson espoused.

In his marvelous introduction to the exhibition catalogue, Johnson gives voice to those principles, extolling geometry over gesture, the gleaming sensuality of industrial materials—glass, ceramics, and steel—the inconsequence of handcraft, the importance of function, and the style inherent in industrial production. Though rigorous, *Machine Art* did not attempt to be comprehensive; though discerning, it did not attempt to be perfect in its connoisseurship; though appreciative of talent, it did not attempt to identify the special gift of any particular design practice. Instead, Johnson took an exquisite snapshot of an emerging visual sensibility, one whose origins could not be traced to any single person, practice, profession, or industry.

Johnson was neither an industrial cheerleader nor a hard-core functionalist, his mannerism manifest in his decided swerve toward aesthetics. Having already noted with consternation the appearance of "much naïve and dreary functionalism," he makes clear that his priority in the show is an appreciation of beauty, and in particular, Beauty in the key of Plato: simple, geometric, rhythmic, elegant. Invoking Thomas Aquinas, "that which being seen, pleases," Johnson writes:

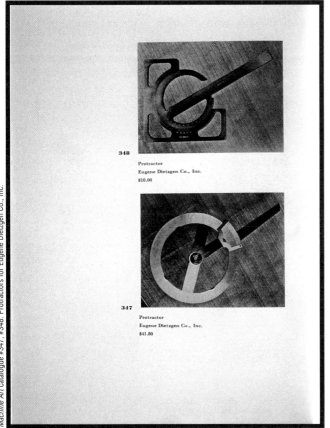

348 Protractor
Eugene Dietzgen Co., Inc.
$10.00

347 Protractor
Eugene Dietzgen Co., Inc.
$41.80

The exhibition contains machines, machine parts, scientific instruments, and objects useful in ordinary life. There are no purely ornamental objects; the useful objects were, however, chosen for their aesthetic quality. Some will claim that usefulness is more important than beauty, or that usefulness makes an object beautiful. This exhibition has been assembled from the point of view that though usefulness is an essential, appearance has at least as great a value.

In Johnson's view, fortune had dropped the power and precision of industrial technology into the lap of a democracy with a relatively wealthy middle class—the raging depression notwithstanding—a perfect formula for distributing the ideal perfection of Platonic forms throughout everyday life. Like others before and since, Johnson got snared in one of modernity's great traps, the desire for timeless ideals to emerge from a world constructed entirely out of the capricious forces of history. Sixty years later, in his preface to a reprint of the *Machine Art* catalogue, Johnson acknowledges as much:

How much has changed! Chaos theory has replaced classic certainties. We prefer Heraclitian flux to Platonic ideas, the principle of uncertainty to the model of perfection, complexity to simplicity. My catalogue text seems juvenile today, … [At the time] Platonic dreams of perfection were the ideal. Complexity and uncertainty were not the aim of the 1934 show.

Thus is the stage set for *Mood River,* with its own vast array of objects, mustered this time, however, to catch the conscience of that flux.

In 1934, each piece exhibited was in and of itself a model of the ideal; whether a glass beaker or a Dietzgen protractor or a Dunhill Meerschaum pipe, each work exemplified the tenets of machine art. Taking that argument to an extreme, then, the exhibition actually only needed one object, its assortment serving but to demonstrate the depth of its unifying aesthetic and its range of congruency. On the other hand, because *Mood River* focuses on flux and flows, no single work is adequate as a model. No list of characteristics can distill the Hold Everything black pencil, the 2001 Porsche Boxster taillight, the Edra *Meditation Pod,* and Ingo Maurer's *Porca Miseria* lamp into examples of a single aesthetic. Rather, to begin to suggest the surprising connections and complex relations that flow through and join such diverse designs, the entire multiplicity of the exhibition's contents is required, much as one needs to bring |together the geology, the climate, and every species of plant and animal of a habitat to grasp the intricate coherence of its ecology. Yet, though *Mood* offers a complex, ever-changing coherence as an alternative to *Machine's* timeless congruency, both share a conviction in a deep unity. Thus, each challenges the prevailing view that sees the world of contemporary design, art, and beyond as an incongruent, incoherent pluralism.

Yet, the *River* did not arise from the *Machine* as a fully formed concept like Athena from the head of Zeus; it did not even spring from it as headwaters, swelling inexorably and inevitably into its currency. Rather, it emerged from a misty inkling in the esoteric ethers of materialist theater, a mere eddy among countless fleeting swirls, one that merely lingered a moment too long. It began to condense, then to grow and evolve, then to discharge outrageous conjectures on the damp mysteries of material practices in contemporary design and art. Like all shows, like all life, its ontogeny recapitulated its phylogeny until, eventually, it found its comic form.

Mood River pokes its fun with a three-pronged fork, each tine suggested by the title. "Mood" proclaims the exhibition's review of the rainbow of contemporary humors, from Serenity to Bliss to Ecstasy to Rage to Trauma and all shades in-between, and its contention that, over and above any prosaic obligation—to function for design, to meaning for art, to fungible interest for both—material practices traffic in those humors. "Mood" signals also the exhibition's most controversial claim: that there are not only new ideas, but new feelings in the world, some fleeting, others more persistent, a claim that in its most radical moment asserts that new ideas are themselves nothing but a particular expression, one among many, of new feelings. To this theme, we shall return.

Let the river pull you under (David Byrne)

"River" indicates the exhibition's fascination with the unfathomable flows that coalesce into each work of art, each work of design, each person, indeed, into each and every thing that exists: flows momentous and minute, flows of matter and organization, of knowledge, technique, and technology, of money, sociology, and politics, and ultimately, flows of desire, so that each and every thing is saturated with a mind-boggling treasure of histories. Condensing for a moment into and as an object, these flows in turn spring from that object-moment anew to feed again the flux of the river. The exhibition telegraphs its preoccupation with these flows above all through its fixation on a peculiar drawing: a Reynolds's diagram.

In 1880, Osborne Reynolds began streaming clear liquids streaked with dye down a glass tube to study the behavior of fluid flow. Three years later, he published his mathematical analysis relating the changing pattern of the streaks to changes in fluid temperature, a cornerstone in the science of fluid mechanics. Still in use today, dye-streaked flow tanks chart the behavior of fluids in motion subject to a wide variety of influences.

In 1977, for reasons far-flung from this exhibition, F. X. Wortmann generated the particular Reynolds's diagram adopted by *Mood River*. It makes visible the evolution of Tollmien-Schlichting waves that begin at the left as smooth, two-dimensional flows, roll up in the middle to become three-dimensional, and finally erupt into turbulence at the right. Of course, though fascinated, we did not care too much about the science, we just fell in love with the image, adopting it as our curatorial instrument, measuring every selection in the show against it, drawing all of our arguments from it, designing the installation around it, making of it not only the symbol, but the *raison d'être* of our efforts.

The more time we spent with the diagram, the more we saw in it the heart and soul of our project; it became our cobra, we its charmers. It not only evoked every mood and contained every shape in the show, from linear to sinuous to voluptuous to chaotic, it seemed to depict every item! We found in it, like castles in the clouds, the Mono cutlery, the David Reed painting, the Hussein Chalayan *Table Dress,* the SIMPARCH *Free Basin* skateboard bowl, and more and more. To our delight, the diagram joined this grab bag of disjoint disparities together, making of each but a moment in a single, dynamic process, our Dharma, our dance of Shiva. But most of all, this hypnotic diagram was achingly beautiful. Why, we wondered? Why do these eddies and vortices seem so gorgeous?

In and of themselves, the flows in our diagram are trivial—liquids, dyes, temperature, the pressure effects caused by the shape of the container. (Though if we give it another thought, these, too, grow more elaborate, for are not the histories of science and mathematics, not to mention the personal history of Osborne Reynolds himself, in some sense flowing in that tube? How, otherwise, did Reynolds happen to put his experiment together, or Wortmann, a hundred years later, his?) Even so, the River diagram offers an elegant portrayal of form not as a timeless idea made manifest in matter, but as an interaction in time among material flows.

In fact, any emphasis on form itself now becomes misleading. The ancient view of things as forms with properties added—weight, color, luminosity, tactility, etc.—gives way to a view of things as condensates, vortices within flows. As long as the interacting flows remain basically stable, the resulting vortex remains more or less persistent, but as soon as a new flow enters, a temperature difference, a new color, a new material, a comet, the vortices reorganize and something new emerges. This view calls us to the hidden histories not just of form but of each flow, to those histories within histories that converge into each current that in turn converges into the machinations of the River.

F. X. Wortmann, Transition downstream of Tollmien-Schlichting waves

Color Samples

May 13, 1969 Internal Memo by Diana Vreeland, Editor, Vogue Magazine
I have just sent in some fake leather to Mrs. Ingersoll from France.
I think it absolutely superb. It comes in every known color. It will
change the course of history.

*

Color and the Princess Telephone ("It's Little, It's Lovely, and it
Lights")
1959–62: white, rose pink, light beige, aqua blue, turquoise
1963–67: add black, moss green, pastel yellow, light grey, special
order in gold
1967–69: add ivory and cherry red
1971–72: drop turquoise and light grey; add clear
mid–80s: add teal blue; production ends
1993–94 revival: white, ivory, pink, peach, powder blue, slate blue,
cameo green

*

In 1859, eighteen-year old chemist William Perkins accidentally
made the first synthetic aniline dye. Adored by France's Empress
Eugénie, who thought it complemented her eyes, Perkins Mauve
generated an unprecedented fashion sensation that swept Europe
and launched the coal tar dye industry, the origin of today's
pharmaceutical, plastics, and dyestuffs industries.

*

Scorned by the Greeks and Romans as ugly and barbaric, banned
from the Carolingian court, deplored, reviled, and vilified, blue was
never even mentioned as a color of the rainbow in natural
philosophy texts spanning more than 1500 years from Aristotle to
Roger Bacon. Then, in just a few short decades at the opening of
the twelfth century, Blue enjoyed a near-miraculous change in
fortunes. The perfection of stained glass and the theological
writings of Abbot Suger conspired to make of it the most revered

and, today, the most popular color in the U.S. and Europe. Abbot
Suger argued that color was immaterial light and therefore divine,
against the opposing view that held color to be a material added to
light, and therefore a profanity sullying divine emanation.

*

Suger oversaw the reconstruction of Saint Denis cathedral, one of
the mid twelfth-century cathedrals such as Vendôme and Chartres
to use blue glass extensively and launch its meteoric rise. Among
his other achievements, Suger wedded blue to gold as the color
combination par excellence to celebrate divine light and the
splendor of creation. The combination reverberates widely today,
notably in the ubiquitous men's double-breasted navy blazer with
brass buttons. Beyond all reasonable explanation, on the other
hand, remains the repulsive inclination to join the navy blazer to
khaki pants, the fashion equivalent of uniting raw oysters with
caramel into Oyster Brittle.

*

In Cleveland, Ohio, in the 1930s, the Switzer brothers—inventors
of Day-Glo paint—began a process that culminated in 1962, when
Lawrence Herbert founded the Pantone Corporation, fountainhead
of color printing and formulation, and Andy Warhol started the
Factory and began the series of prints whose colors and color
combinations would change the spectrum of our world forever.

*

Products today, from pens to furniture to kitchen sinks, tend to be
offered in five or more colors, with a nod toward transparency,
making the five-flavor Life Saver candy roll a veritable archetype of
contemporary design. Clarence Crane, who invented the Life Saver
in 1912 in Garrettsville, Ohio, introduced the five-flavor pack in 1935.

**More and more, today, we find awe and delight in these hidden
histories. Physicists tell us that a supernova, an aged star's last rage
against the dying of the light, threw off the matter that makes up our
earth and everything on it, including us. "We are stardust," Joni
Mitchell wrote in her song, "Woodstock," and she meant it, which is
why her words are engraved on a marble bench outside the Princeton
University Department of Physics. The open-air settings, the vigorous
brushstrokes and knife work, and the brilliant colors and ephemeral
light effects that transformed some of that stardust into Impressionist
paintings are inconceivable before the early-nineteenth-century
development of thickened paint preparations, the invention of tubed
paint and portable easels, and the replacement of round brushes by
flat ones made possible by the development of metal ferrules.
Impressionism is a magnificent vortex born out of the intercourse
between the history of painterly ideas and the lives of its artists. But
within that vortex writhe myriad eddies of cosmology, technology,
chemistry, and invention.**

**Can you sense how deep, how very deep this River runs? The
change from a world of forms to a world of flows, a candidate for**

the very definition of modernity itself, courses through the most radical, counter-intuitive signposts of our own becoming, through the philosophy of Hegel, the history of Marx, the biology of Darwin, the psychology of Freud, the physics of Bohr and Einstein, the geology of Wegener, the art of Picasso and Pollock, the cosmology of Gamow and Guth, and neither last nor least, the glorious furniture of Panton.

The *Panton Chair* stands as the avatar and *éminence colorée* of the exhibition, its bloodlines detectable throughout the waterfall of chairs and beyond, from its direct descendants, such as the carbon-fiber Pagnotta *Z Chair,* to the one-piece, folded paper chairs by Polyline. The first chair made in one piece from entirely synthetic materials, the *Panton Chair* began life in 1961 as a sheath of sketches and a polysteron prototype suitable for seeing, but not sitting. After years of exhibitions, further prototyping, and negotiations with various manufacturers, the chair finally received its first limited production run by Herman Miller in collaboration with Vitra in 1967, with 150 cold-pressed, fiberglass-reinforced polyester chairs, hand lacquered and finished.

Verner Panton, its designer, disliked the laborious production process, the heavy weight, the uneven finish, and the high cost, though he was pleased that the chair's appearance on the cover of the Italian design magazine *Mobile* launched it to instant, worldwide stardom. A year later, Panton shifted to Baydur, a polyurethane hard-foam produced by the Bayer corporation, bringing the costs down by making the molding process easier. Though still manually spackled, sanded, and painted, the polyeurethane gave a smoother, shiny surface, better captured the sleek lines, and allowed the thickness of shell to vary according to the structural demands on various parts of the chair. In 1971 production shifted to Luran S, a thermoplastic styrene that was injection molded and required no hand finishing, yielding a much less expensive chair. Injection technology at the time allowed only for shells of uniform thickness, so the graceful modulation in structural thickness gave way to reinforcement ribbing. Prone to breakage, the chair engendered the mistrust of consumers and cast a pall on the entire field of plastic furniture; production ceased in 1979.

Unwilling to let its star fade away, Vitra resumed production in 1983 with a return to polyurethane and the claim that the new chair, in its third official manifestation, was indistinguishable from the 1968–70 model, save for a Panton signature stamped on the base. In the thirteen years between the first and second polyurethane versions,

however, the formulation of the finishing paint had changed color saturation and hue, and aficionados have no difficulty in distinguishing chairs from the two periods, though they debate over their preferences. Finally, in 1999, Vitra introduced a fourth authorized version in injection-molded polypropylene that retained the contoured thickness and met almost all the original wishes of Panton: inexpensive, light, even color, no hand finishing. All save one: prone to scratches, the new chair, exhibited in *Mood River*, must be produced in a matte finish. Edgar Allen Poe would have preferred this finish, no doubt. He wrote in his *Philosophy of Furniture*, "glare is a leading error in the philosophy of American Household decoration, we are violently enamored of gas and glass."

Four minor changes in material flow, four slightly different chairs, four perceptibly different evocations, each with its own devotees. Those attached to one treat others as imposters, like fans of the real James Bond. "History, does not repeat itself," Twain quipped, "but sometimes it rhymes."

Imagine, now, that life around town is but one big Reynolds's tube, its floodgate open wide to all of the flows that shape, organize, and reorganize matter: histories galore, new materials, new technologies, new stories, new appetites, fears, and desires, money, politics, world affairs. Today, as we consider the extent to which new materials, computer-aided design and manufacturing, just-in-time inventory methods, and the other astonishing achievements of science, technology, business, management, and marketing collude not only to speed up but to liquefy contemporary material life, are we and everything around us not just one big Reynolds's diagram?

OK, maybe not, but you get the point, don't you?

Moon River (Henry Mancini and Johnny Mercer)
For the third prong of its fork, *Mood River* alludes to the dreamy theme song for the 1961 film version of *Breakfast at Tiffany's*, with just a hint of "Moody River," Pat Boone's chart-topping ballad of tragic love from the same year. The allusion draws attention to the exhibition's fascination with music and in particular to a special case of the power of music over mood: the soundtrack effect. By operating in the realm of distracted attention, behind those aspects of a film that insist on close attention such as the acting and the plot, the soundtrack gains sway over mood, manipulating the viewer's feeling about a scene. Recall the relentless disquiet wrought by the turning, unresolved arpeggios in Bernard Hermann's score for Hitchcock's *Vertigo*, an effect intensified and updated with a psychopathic edge with Kubrick's brilliant appropriation of Ligeti's 1951 two-note piano drone, Musica Ricercata No. 2, in the filmmaker's *Eyes Wide Shut*. Or simply consider Audrey Hepburn's note to Mancini:

> Dear Henry,
>
> I have just seen our picture—BREAKFAST AT TIFFANY'S—this time with your score. A movie without music is a little like an aeroplane without fuel. However beautifully the job is done, we are still on the ground and in a world of reality. Your music has lifted us all up and sent us soaring. Everything we cannot say with words or show with action you have expressed for us. You have done this with so much imagination, fun and beauty.
>
> You are the hippest of cats—and the most sensitive of composers!
>
> Thank you, dear Hank.
>
> Lots of love, Audrey

Always at work beneath close attention, design operates as the visual "soundtrack" for everyday life.

The relationship music constructs between the expertise of the composer/performer and the mood of the listener in many ways corresponds to that between the expert practice of a designer and the response his work engenders. If you, too, well with tears each time you hear Pavarotti render Puccini's "Nessun Dorma," though you have no idea what the Italian lyrics mean, then you know already the direct power of music over feelings. Like a designer responding to a functional program, Puccini first studied the text of the librettist in minute detail, analyzing the story, the action, the meaning and nuance of the words, as well as their rhythms, inflections, and sonorities. Relying on his detailed, technical knowledge of music as much as on inspiration, he worked as if to derive the composition from the inherent musicality of the lyrics themselves. By the time he finished, however, the effect of his efforts on the emotions of the listener so transcends its initial commitment to the story and lyrics that it takes on a life of its own. Many know the libretto and they no doubt enjoy the aria to its fullest, but many more are deeply touched, though they have no inkling of the curious story of Turandot, nor why the tenor sings, "no one sleeps." In much the same way, every design, whether intended expressly to stimulate passions, such as Ross Lovegrove's *Go Chair,* or driven seemingly by functional considerations alone, such as Enron's 750kw wind turbine blade, transcends its functional program to evoke an emotional response. James Corner, award-winning landscape architect and critic, calls the wind turbine fields in southern California, Iowa, and Texas "the most beautiful works of landscape art in the Nation."

Is it right for *Mood River* to ignore function? Without a doubt, the functional achievements of the various product designs in the show deserve admiration. Who would not wish for cleaner teeth, healthier gums, sharper knives, safer helmets, faster juicers, more-agile skateboards? The exhibition does not diminish function, it merely claims that appeal itself is a paramount function. The engineering of better dental hygiene and gum care that motivates the brilliant design of the Aquafresh Flex toothbrush—matched by other, equally compelling innovations in the Colgate, Crest, Oral B, and other major toothbrush brands—provides an interesting case.

The designers of the Aquafresh Flex choreographed a stunning *pas de deux* of hard and soft plastics to produce a performance jewel. The hard plastic acts as the active spine for the entire brush, while the soft plastic adds the flesh, from body to cushioning joint. At the base, the hard plastic provides the armature for the fleshy, soft-plastic handle; as the hard spine moves towards the head, it thins and tapers, then ripples into a spring-like shock absorber, its spaces filled by cushioning soft-plastic. Finally, just before the hard plastic widens to complete the platform for the bristles, it breaks like a spinal vertebrate to allow an insert gasket of soft plastic to become a flexible joint, ostensibly to protect the gums from abrasion. (The amazing duet between the two plastics is made all the more beautiful as the hard plastic inscribes in profile and by sheer luck, a faithful sketch of the *Mood River* diagram!) Now, independent studies of the Aquafresh and other premium performance toothbrushes indicate that, as instruments of dental hygiene, they work very well, but not measurably better than traditional designs. On the other hand, the same studies show that the toothbrush's attractiveness, comfort, and design aura cause them to be used more regularly by their owners, improving dental health.

Even if appeal deserves our attention as a mode of performance, is it fair, one might ask, to equate one intentionally evocative design with the incidental effects of another, to compare, that is, the feelings stimulated by the *Go Chair* with those awakened as a mere by-product by the Enron wind turbine blade, a question central to *Machine Art.* Alfred Barr, in his foreword, struggled with the question:

> The beauty of machine art in so far as it is a mere by-product of function may seem a meagre and even trivial kind of beauty. But this is not necessarily so. The beauty of all natural objects is also a by-product—the helix of a snail's shell (and a steel coil), the graduated feathering of a bird's wing (and the leaves of a laminated spring), the rabbit's footprints in the snow (and the track of non-skid tires), the elegance of fruit (and of incandescent bulbs.)

The issue becomes even more evident in the *River.* State-of-the-art industrial production in the 1930s favored simple forms, glass and metal, casting, milling, turning and presswork, and assembly line processing that combined simple elements into kit-of-part, composite designs. A brief harmony of scales, unperceived at the time but apparent in retrospect, lent itself to the ethic of modern design. The dimensions of functioning parts, the usable size of the end product, the physical properties of the materials, the scale of the modeling, drawing, and detailing in the design process, the methods of production and distribution, and the prices all converged, more or less, to the same order. Take, for example, Henry Dreyfuss's classic black cradle telephone for AT&T, a pioneering example of ergonomic industrial design. The electrical and mechanical works just filled the Bakelite case and handle, which just fit the hand, ear, and mouth, and was just the right size and weight to manage, package, and deliver at a cost that made leasing plausible. From ball bearings to tools to radios and televisions to washing machines to printing presses, this conver-gence of scales yielded a remarkable correspondence of form, function, production, price, and marketing.

Over the seven decades since, technologies have coevolved to revolutionize industrial production, transforming it from solid processing to fluid processing. Microprocessor electronics, material science and chemistry, computer-aided design, and robotic, computer-driven manufacturing methods have rent asunder the scale harmonies of modernism. In the endless variety of today's telephone, a thimbleful of miniaturized chips replaces the boxful of wires, contact switches, and bells in the Dreyfuss phone, forever repealing any law of necessity between contents and case. Meanwhile, CAD programs give the designer point-by-point control of the shape of the entire surface, and computer-driven injection molding, thermoforming, abrasive jet, ion beam, and laser machining manipulate materials at an ever-finer scale to realize the designer's fantasy. The strength, ductility, lightness, and behavior of the plastics, ceramics, composite resins, gels, alloys, and other new materials are such that they are often termed "smart," even "intelligent," much to my envy and that of most of my friends. Manufacture tends more towards redirecting flows and deforming plugs and away from forging, machining, and assembling simple parts.

Pick from the *River*'s cornucopia a provisional selection: Charles Debbas's *ErgoPen*, Philippe Starck's *xO* dumbbells, Frank Gehry's proposed high-rise for Times Square, Giro's *Pneumo* bike safety helmet, Issey Miyake's *Colombe* dress, and Siobhán Hapaska's *Land* sculpture. Is their undulating similarity not uncanny, though produced by very different means and directed towards very different ends? The *ErgoPen* joins bioengineering and ergonomic analysis, computer modeling and gas-assist injection molding to make an affordable pen that fits comfortably into either a left- or right-handed writing grip. Striving for style, aerodynamics, ventilation, and lightness but above all safety, the Giro helmet uses high-impact polycarbonate plastic wrapped around a soft EPP foam core, in-molded to a wind-swept geodesic structure. To make his alluring model of the proposal for Times Square, Frank Gehry gathers and drapes metal mesh over a wood frame like a dressmaker, while dressmaker cum architect Issey Miyake cuts small vents into a single rectangle woven in monofilament nylon for his *Colombe* dress, which acquires its glistening, sinuous undulations as the rectangle warps reluctantly around the body, a curtain wall trying to become a dress. Siobhán Hapaska hand sculpts polysterene foam into a mold, casts it in fiberglass, polishes, paints, and coats it in acrylic to produce her mysterious *Land*, whose fusion of serenity and anxiety grows out of its simultaneous suggestion of an ancient rock, smoothed by eons of ebbs and flows of tides, and some futuristic vehicle forged out of some as-yet-unknown metal, a disturbing rumor made visible.

However diverse the design and production method, in each case a portion of pliant matter deforms under the influence of impinging forces to yield an erotic object. Whatever its primary intended use, the materiality, shape, and surface of that object join with memory, context, and expectation to evoke mood. Sometimes, the deforming forces at work are vectors of scientific analysis and manufacturing process, sometimes of artistic intuition and manipulation, sometimes merely of gravity. Yet, in each and every case, the erotics of the object—that cocktail of desire, revulsion, and fear it stirs—is an *index* of the transformation of matter by information through force toward effect.

Introduced at the end of the nineteenth century by Charles Peirce as part of his attempt to formulate a semiotics, a theory of meaning, the basic idea of an index is simple enough, even if it eventually gives rise to mind-twisting consequences. When a pebble hits a windshield and cracks it, or hits the door of the car and dents it, or hits your head and puts a knot on it, the cracks, dent, and knot are each an index of a similar event. An index indicates the event as evidence more than representing it in the manner of a sign or symbol. Unlike signs and symbols that are more or less independent of specific materiality—one can tap out Morse code for "cat" on a radio or a drum, draw a cat in paint or pencil, say or write the word "cat"—the materiality of the indexical effect is crucial, as the difference between cracked glass, dented sheet metal, and a knot on the head suggests. Indeed, even as we recognize the same "cat" in each of our six instances of representation, we also recognize that each instance "feels" different and communicates a host of information and sensations distinct from one another, a consequence of the indexical specificity of each case. We don't love James Mason's or Tom Waits's English, we love the accent, the rhythm, and the elocution; we love, that is, the indexical effects of each voice.

Whenever forces act on matter, vocal chords on air, for example, they generate indices, but the magic arises with the effects these indices engender. As we have seen already in the Reynolds's diagram, indexical effects have a strange power to beguile, to intrigue, to speak directly to emotions. Always potent, always mesmerizing to be sure—but let us not create the false impression that indexical effects are always appealing. Perhaps the single plug of semi-fluidic matter most saturated with and organized by information in the universe, the human brain abounds in indexical effects, its slimy gray mounds and crevices a reliable source of disgust.

Indexical effects are the stuff of individuality, identity, and character, so much so that the legal force of a signature turns not on its power to represent a name through letters, but entirely on the identifiable specificity of its marks, that is, on the indexical idiosyncrasies of a person's handwriting. Aesthetic pleasure, mood, and atmosphere belong to the family of indexical effects, inevitable whether or not the indexical effect itself is the originally intended goal. Johnson's and Barr's defense of the relative merit of incidental versus intentional beauty amounts in retrospect to an appreciation of indexical effects, of their ubiquity, range, and power, but they were far from the first. Some 300 years earlier Leonardo da Vinci wrote:

> It is not to be despised, in my opinion, if, after gazing fixedly at the spot on the wall, the coals in the grate, the clouds, the flowing stream, if one remembers some of their aspects. If you look at them carefully, you will discover some quite admirable inventions. Of these, the genius of the painter may take full advantage…

And the consequences of indexical effects are by no means limited to the worlds of art and design. In his most recent book, *Investigations*, biologist and complexity theorist Stuart Kaufmann elaborates on Stephen J. Gould's notion of the "exaptation" to locate indexical effects at the very heart of the diversifying power of evolutionary processes. An exaptation is, in brief, an incidental feature of an organism that elevates into a survival adaptation as the environment changes.

Most indexical effects are incidental. The peculiar lozenge shapes of the taillights in *Mood River*, for example, are as much a consequence of their being clipped by a trunk edge or required to maintain a quarter-panel line as a sculptural decision on the part of a designer. The fascination exercised by the Lockheed F-117A Stealth Fighter, code named Have Blue during its top secret development, is another case in point. The team of engineers and scientists who designed the plane had but one thing in mind, one effect: a functioning fighter with zero radar profile—period. Yet, as they saturated their materials with more information, it began to radiate with indexicality: its black, diamond-faceted, wasp-waisted specter arrests all who see it. Not long after it appeared, the awkward, faceted geometry of the plane spread like a virus into other domains of design: its influence is readily apparent, for example in Ben van Berkel's *Fragile* platter, Kivi Sotamaa's *Extraterrain* chair, Giovanni Pagnotta's desk lamp and Peter Eisenman's proposal for the Church of the Year 2000.

For centuries, artists and designers have followed Leonardo, drawing inspiration from found incidental effects, even, in the twentieth century, formalizing their production of these with chance methods and other processes. Yves Klein's painting by dipping nudes in blue and having them stir about on a canvas comes to mind. In recent years, a more disciplined, systematic use of information to generate indexical effects has been explored in art by Sol LeWitt, for example, and in architecture by Peter Eisenman. The architect achieved the striking resemblance between his Church for the Year 2000 and the Stealth Fighter, for example, not by imitation, but by mirroring the processes of a liquid-crystal folding to generate his design. Sotamaa worked in a similar vein, though his appeal to aircraft was more direct. To design the ET chair, he sampled 3-D forms from a library of American military aircraft models, organized the samples in a relief map on a computer, printed the map in Styrofoam as a prototype, then sculpted and tested for further development.

We must take care not to suggest that indexical effects are either reproducibly stable or purely optical, as if some chart could correlate precise combinations of form, color, and luminosity to specific moods and feelings, though the effort to produce such a chart is as old as the philosophy of art itself. The problem is richer, more complicated. While indexical effects are distinct from symbolic and signifying effects, for example, one can never simply be separated from the other; indeed, they slip into one another. Why? At least in part because language, history, context, and information, the stuff of meaning, also act as forces that manipulate matter, while gesture, texture, color, and the other emotive residues of manipulated matter in turn can become signs and symbols. If Yves Klein's nudes amplified the indexical sensuality of the brushstroke, Roy Lichtenstein transformed that brushstroke into symbol, as does Rich Little when he mimics the voices of Hollywood stars.

A peacock struts up, plumage in full macho display. A birdwatcher sees decorative beauty, a peahen sees beefcake, a nearby peacock sees an asshole beggin' for a beatin', and a hawk sees dinner. Each partitions the same processed matter, the image of the bird, into signal and noise. Each pays close attention to the signal, allowing the leftover noise to slip in almost unnoticed through distracted attention, like the soundtrack of a film. And each partitions the same image differently: what is signal to one is noise to another. In order, the signifying/feeling pairs are bird/admiration, mate/arousal, rival/anger, food/hunger. Meanings and feelings separate, but in each case, separate differently.

A rare disorder called Capgras syndrome offers a glimpse into the distinct pathways of feelings and ideas. Sufferers of Capgras endure the nightmare of feeling that the people and things closest to them—their parents, spouses, children, pets, even their houses and contents—have been replaced by imposters. Long treated as a psychotic delusion, the mystery of Capgras was solved in recent years by the brilliant neuroscientist Vilyanur Ramachandran, who discovered that the recognition of a loved one is a two-fold process: an identification by the visual centers in the temporal lobe and an assessment of emotional value by the amygdala, gateway to the brain's limbic system, seat of the emotions. In the Capgras patient, the neural link between the amygdala and the temporal lobe is physically broken. Thus, he recognizes his mother, but does not feel the appropriate emotional confirmation. It is as if, to recall the joke by comedian Stephen Wright, the patient came home and everything he owned was stolen and replaced by an exact duplicate.

The slippery mobility of meanings and feelings shapes design history in unexpected ways. The early-modern predilection for simple lines, stainless steel, and white lingered in hospitals, medical products, and products for the differently-abled long after color and gesture began to enliven other product sectors. The aesthetic pleasures of early modernism congealed for a particular group into a sign-system representing clinical sobriety, as if to say that a person under stress should no longer be subject to the frivolity of design. After decades

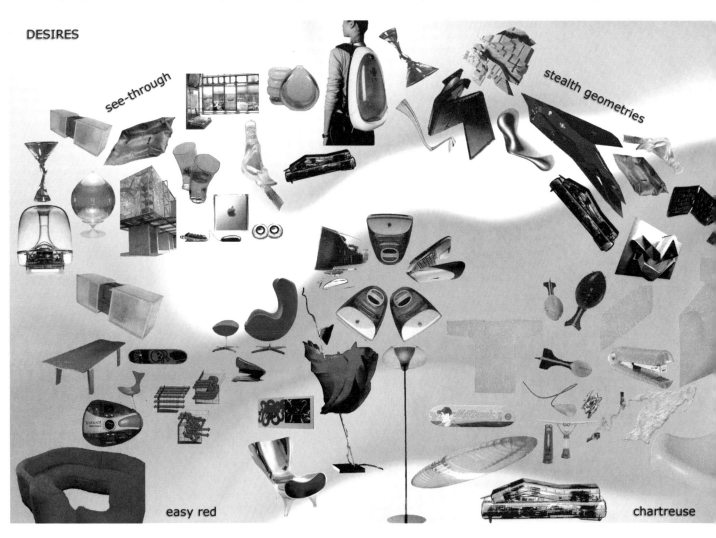

DESIRES

see-through

stealth geometries

easy red

chartreuse

serene   sinuous   voluptuous   chaotic

of plaints from a clientele excluded from the delights of design, the situation finally turned a corner as medical supply companies joined the general culture of design, offering everything from injectors to inhalers to electronic monitors in eye-catching shapes and candy-store colors, while sporty wheelchairs rival motorcycles for flair. What motivates the new wave of medical design, however, is less a matter of altruism than a lesson learned long ago by Madison Avenue, another instance of identity collaborating with emotion, marketing's favorite version of a familiar face: brand loyalty.

I second that emotion (Smokey Robinson)

Mood River, of course, is nothing more than an exhibition of design and art, a party for the eye spiced with tall tales of flows and vortices and indexical effects, as remote from the rigors of science as it can get. Nothing more, but also nothing less. Still, it harbors a secret fantasy to say something about mood and atmosphere, feelings, and emotions. Though scientists, sociologists, and anthropologists may study these elusive efflorescences, it is art, design, and their siblings—music, dance, literature, poetry, and theater—that muster them into a world, with the help of technology. Play is the thing.

And to make a claim that some will find dubious: That new feelings erupt into the world, that design and the arts give diverse and specific material moment to these new feelings, help make them choate and concrete, and spread them about like the wind spreads pollen, like mosquitoes spread disease. After these new feelings have materialized, taken shape, taken various shapes, and disseminated, they eventually evolve into their most auspicious incarnation as new ideas.

Clearly, the stuff around us effects our feelings and our moods. We wash our hands and face and feel refreshed. We put on a formal tux or gown and we feel formal. In a kilt, we feel foolish, unless we are Highlanders, in which case the tux/kilt effect is reversed. House clean = feel good. (Scientist have proven that for obscure reasons, men are physiologically able to remember this relationship only after the fact.) Studies show that average productivity drops in offices on casual Friday. The sun sets, the music lingers, the perfume wafts, the couch plushes or whatever couches do, and the next thing you know…, well, you know.

But *new* feelings? The big bang theory and the theory of evolution, for those of us who subscribe, insist that at some point all feelings—love, envy, heartbreak, chocolate ecstasy—were new. First there was matter, then life, then human life, then hot fudge; somewhere along the line each of our feelings emerged for the first time. Yet, that only argues that all our current feelings were new at some time; what suggests that new feelings keep coming on line?

Till you were six or seven or eight, you and your mom kinda' liked the same music, Mr. Rogers singing inky dinky spider or Garth Brooks or Alice Cooper, whatever. Then, one day, you go to a friend's house and come home wearing a mullet, listening to Jimmy Eat World, and looking for a stereo system with a volume control that goes to 11. The hair feels like the real you; the music feels cool, touches you deep, speaks to you, for you. Finally, you can actually hear that numbing rhythm and cranky squeal that has been floating around the back of your head for a while, and it sounds great. Your mom, on the other hand, says, "I'll be damned if you're wearing that haircut in this house, and cut that junk off, it's not music, it's…, it's…, it's junk! You're driving me crazy!" Welcome to day one of a really bad decade to come.

What happened? According to our story, you and your mom were roughly in the same persistent flow state when measured on matters of music, until, eventually, the vortex that is you accumulated enough new flows—different experiences, personal relationships, things—that it reorganized you into a different state, one with new feelings experienced as new tastes in music and hairstyles. Sensations that cause mom genuine discomfort cause you genuine pleasure. You diverge from your mom toward your friend. Noteworthy is the fact that, though no idea has been formulated or exchanged, the reorganization by taste is essentially political. One party, you and mom, bifurcates into two, your mom and persons of her taste, versus you and your friend. Be sure, the contest of ideas will soon follow.

But why are these new feelings, why not just the recombination of old feelings? Indeed, they are a recombination, but then, again, we need a second look at combinations. In one possibility, the kit-of-parts model we recall from the discussion of works in the *Machine Art* show, each element of a combination remains identifiably intact and contributes to the contribution as such—as in a mechanical device or a collage, for example. In another, the fluid vortex model of combination, the identity and properties of each of the components are effaced as they merge into something new. In these, the resulting organization itself is new, with new properties that do not belong to the old. A tornado is not a version of the winds that precede it, water not a sum of the properties of hydrogen and oxygen. Pink, a combination of red and white, is a new color in its own right, one that acts on its own and gives rise to further developments: hot pink, blush, coral. *Pink and blue* is not a condensed version of *red, white, and blue.*

In the 1660s, the microscope spread like wildfire around Europe, the cell phone of its day. In the restaurants of London and Paris, precociously successful young merchants and accountants would pull out their new microscopes and start looking at the food, much to the irritation of patrons with finer manners. In 1674, Leibniz invented differential calculus, the mathematics of the infinitesimal, a microscopic look at a curve. An accident? We think not. Now, take a second look at that weird new chair you bought. Without your ever quite being aware of it, in a few weeks or so it will show up in your dreams, a few months later in your idle thoughts, then, not long after, in your ideas. Behind every Nobel Prize stands an impulse purchase!

In his book *The Feeling of What Happens*, neurologist Antonio Damasio writes of six universal emotions: happiness, sadness, fear, anger, surprise, and disgust. Damasio draws on the work of psychologist Paul Ekman, who demonstrated that basic facial expressions for each of these are common to all cultures. Damasio goes on to relate fundamental emotions and their common expressions to the possibility of cross-cultural communications and to the capacity of the arts in particular to cross frontiers, a mobility more immediately enjoyed by indexical and representational effects than by signifying effects. Which is to say nothing more than that a painting travels easier than a poem.

He then turns to secondary emotions, such as embarrassment, jealousy, guilt, and pride, secondary not because they are less important, but because they arise out of social conditioning and differ more from context to context. (So far, the reading is a bit depressing, since seven out of ten of the emotions discussed are unpleasant, and that's only true if you count Pride as pleasant and risk eternal damnation. Fortunately, most of the time we do not feel these emotions as such.) Ultimately, Damasio's main interest, and ours, is in what he calls "background emotions" such as bummed, groovy, chipper, or on edge. According to the author, these provide a more or less "faithful index of momentary parameters of inner organism state."

Damasio: "When we sense that a person is 'tense', 'edgy',… or 'cheerful', without a single word having been spoken to translate any of those possible states, we are detecting background emotions. We detect [and express] background emotions by subtle details of body posture, speed, and contour of movements, minimal changes in the amount and speed of eye movements, and in the degree of contraction of the facial muscles," i.e., as indexical effects perceived through distracted awareness.

Ekman: "Human facial muscles allow more than ten thousand different facial appearances; and the action of these muscles is so rapid that these expressions could all be shown in a few hours. The face sends messages about such transient events as a feeling or emotion, or more enduring moods, and stable personality characteristics…."

Always at work behind its blunt communication of identity, the evocative powers of the face provide the best argument for the claims of *Mood River*, as its fluidity of form, colors, and surface give nuanced expression to feelings, old and new, fleeting and persistent, local and universal, and give rise to these feelings in others. To exaggerate these effects in the design products featured in *Mood River*, we strip away the identity of the products by installing them in unexpected orientations and arrangements: a galaxy of lights, a school of fish of household goods, a coral reef of taillights, a waterfall of chairs, a vortex of sporting goods, all with one end in mind, to tune in and listen as indexical effects strum our hearts with lullabies and power chords.

PS: Send in the Clowns (Sondheim)

"Good machine art is entirely independent of painting, sculpture and architecture."—Alfred Barr, *Machine Art* catalogue foreword

His logic seems impeccable: function, anonymity, and the effacement of expressive handcraft were the essence of machine art. Nevertheless, Barr's declaration rings shrill in the otherwise mellifluous prose of his thoughtful foreword. Barr knew better than most that by 1934 artists and architects in Europe and the United States had been experimenting with the ethic of machine art for over two decades under the influence of the Bauhaus in Germany and *L'Esprit Nouveau* in France. His categorical exclusion of art, therefore, suggests other motives. Reading the texts and reviewing the contents of the show, one imagines a tension on this point between Barr and Johnson, as if a disagreement had occurred behind the scenes and Barr decided to have the last word. Whether or not such a dispute actually happened, Johnson subtly suggests his doubts about Barr's position by grounding machine art in the history of art and architecture and the philosophy of beauty.

Mood River's deep refrain that a coherence flows through the apparent diversity of material life requires a foray into the fine arts. All the more, because, while fine art in the 1920s and 1930s envied the smart, cold, objective precision of machine art and the promise of a better future it engendered, the design in *Mood River* envies the gestural and expressive freedom and emotional range historically enjoyed by the fine arts.

The excursion must be taken with caution, for whatever his reasons, an intelligence underwrites Barr's peremptory categorical exclusion. The fine arts and design are different species of material practice each with its own niche in our cultural ecology. Because design is a pack animal, it needs to like and to be liked; like a puppy, it seeks to fit in, to please, to do tricks. Art, like a cat, is more aloof; solitary, with more mysterious things on its mind, it is willing to be loved but unwilling to broach the slightest compromise to earn love. We approach, encounter, treat, and relate to each differently, and each, in its turn, behaves differently. Where design may explore indexical effects, it is content to work through distracted attention. Art, on the other hand, distills, condenses, and intensifies such effects, presenting them to close attention to drive the thoughts, associations, and feelings of its lover to a singular pitch.

To follow the *River* as it flows into art, to catch connections as eddies of matter and technique swerve from art to design and back, this difference must be respected and preserved. A fatal flaw occurs when art and design enter the same space and the differences between them collapses into a mess. Perhaps that is what Barr rightly feared, considering how often it has happened in exhibitions since. Or perhaps his caution stemmed simply from the daunting magnitude of the undertaking. How does one sample fine art on the questions of material specificity, technique, feeling, and indexical effect without inevitably committing grievous errors of omission? Is not fine art in all of its modes, from painting and sculpture to literature and poetry to theater and music, nothing othe`r than the field of inquiry most dedicated to these very questions themselves? In painting alone, how dare one mention mood without Ross Bleckner, materials without Julian Schnabel, flows and vortices without Karin Davies? In the end, what work of art does not belong in *Mood River*?

It gets even stickier. The assertion of a fundamental distinction between fine art and design has long been controversial and hotly contested by both artists and designers. From dada to Bauhaus to pop art to neo-geo to a host of talented, intelligent young artists experimenting with other cross-over tactics today, a considerable and sustained effort has been made to destabilize the disciplinary boundaries here invoked. Artists such as Jorge Pardo operate at the cusp of art and architecture in a concerted effort to blur the distinctions.

Yet, for all of their wit, their fondness for the everyday, their appropriation of industrial and commercial production, Duchamp's *Fountain*, Johns's Ale Cans, Koons's *Large Vase of Flowers*, and Pardo's Dia bookstore each require two supplements to nourish their very survival as art: reflective close attention and an art-world context. Without museums and galleries and art magazines, *Fountain* would just be a urinal and *A Large Vase of Flowers* a vase of artificial flowers, albeit one curiously fabricated in painted wood. This is not to argue against the significance of each work. To the contrary, these are some of the most cunning works of art in existence, unmatched in their power to make us newly aware of our world and its invisible processes. Rather, it is merely to identify the ineradicable necessity of context, of habitat for any species to survive.

In our quest to explore the migrations of sensibility and mood, we avoided such artworks precisely because, like sharks, they hover so close to design, feeding off it in order to call attention to and critique the social and economic forces that operate covertly through it. Without doubt, these works, too, are subject to flows, they display indexical effects and induce emotions. It might even be said that one of newest feelings on the block—shall we call it "cold-hearted easy"—is the bread and butter of Koons and his kindred. But sharks and aquarium fish in the same tank? Too dangerous; pretty soon, everything would end up Shark.

To be sure, *Mood River* includes artists exploring crossover tactics: Rachael Neubauer's nod to jewelry, Siobhán Hapaska's to furniture, Enlai Hooi's to interior architecture. E. V. Day's stop-action sculpture *Bombshell* draws on film, freeze-frame, and fashion to capture a moment in an explosion of a replica of Marilyn Monroe's icon White Dress from *The Seven Year Itch*, originally created by Oscar-winning costume designer Bill Travilla. Tony Cragg's mesmerizing *Clear Glass Stack,* of plate glass and bottles lets loose a breezy blend of associations and dizzying light effects—flavored with just a pinch of breakage anxiety. David Reed's painting traps the deep-space carved by the decorative flourish of a knifed arabesque within the razor-thin space delimited by graphic design colors. Fabian Marcaccio turns machine guns into paintbrushes—actually, into four-color printers—with his *Paint-Ball Robot.* Unlike their more aggressive critical cousins, each of these works in its own way is at play, indulging the indexical and exploring the evocative.

Confident and urbane, these art works are at ease with design, neither indenturing it nor suffering diminished impact in its quotidian presence. Imagine a bar scene: Ingo Maurer's chandelier, *Porca Miseria,* chats with *Bombshell* on the merits of the exploded field. At another table, David Reed's painting tussles with Hussein Chalayan's *Topiary Dress* and John Chamberlain's *Rubber Comedy*. The three stand arm in arm on color and gesture, but argue heatedly on the dress's blithe use of a flower figure. The rough-hewn, gravel-voiced *Rubber Comedy* baits his younger friends for their refined, prissy finish, pushing a little too hard, all the while muttering under his breath, between sips, about the days when art mattered; when it really mattered. It still does, the Reed and the Chalayan almost dare to say, but at the last minute, change their minds. The simmering *Paint-Ball Robot* sits quietly, listens and wonders.

Frank Stella's *Die Kurfürstin* sits at the table with Gehry's *Horse's Head* and Miyake's *Colombe* dress. Lively and engaged, he nevertheless fidgets a little, unable to bring himself to pretend that the similarities the three share are worth more than a moment's notice. *Kurfürstin* admires the accomplishments of his tablemates, but he cannot and will not equate them with the project undertaken by abstraction. Abstract art drinks in the totalities of other art, absorbs the vicissitudes of a lifetime, its boredoms, traumas, and ecstasies, then materializes that entire life in a single existential gesture. So what if design and art exchange matter or effect? Manure and flowers exchange matter and effect, too. Nothing else scales the heights of abstract art. Anyway, he thinks to himself, these parties come and go; no harm done. And maybe he'll get a chance to talk with *Rubber Comedy* later, he has some thoughts he would like run by his old friend.

Jeffrey Kipnis, an architectural critic, theorist, and designer, is Curator of Architecture and Design at the Wexner Center for the Arts and Professor of Architecture at the Knowlton School of Architecture, The Ohio State University.

My first brush with the idea of "Everyday Brilliance" came in the mid-nineties while at my desk editing pages of *I.D. Magazine*, which I did for a number of years in the last millennium. On one of those hectic, gun-to-the-head days, a contributing writer walked into my office with a grimy paper sack and spilled the contents in front of me. It looked like a pile of trash. What's up with the garbage on my desk? I asked. Look at it, he said. I did. And it was beautiful. Stunningly beautiful trash.

I am deeply grateful to author Phil Patton for that eye-opening moment. What he'd brought me was a stack of cheap plastic coffee cup lids that reify the spectacular American concept of "To Go." (Go where? It doesn't matter. Just luxuriate in the conceptual possibilities, matched only by another great American phenomenon: "While You Wait." But those are other stories.) That morning Phil had literally scooped the collection of lids off the floor of his car (caffeine and cars were made for each other, he explained) and brought them to the office for appraisal.

The lids came in a variety of configurations, of which there were a surprising number. Yet the disks had common characteristics. Cut from rolled polystyrene sheets, crimped with curves and lips for strength, and folded and lapped to fit snuggly over the cups, they were uniform in size and served essentially the same function: to make hot liquid transportable, if not consumable while in motion. Beyond that, they were vastly diverse. Some were scored to provide tearable flaps that fold back for sipping in transit while others were highly engineered with sculpted spouts and extra loft to protect the foam of upscale cappuccinos. And then there were the didactic lids with raised lettering to indicate whether the contents were "Decaf" or "Other" along with mysterious symbols that could mean recycle or perhaps the opposite.

Each was highly precise, and upon further research we learned that a few dozen patents were claimed by the collection.

These lowly objects, the cast-away detritus of many morning commutes, ended up on the cover of my next issue. That was the start of my quest to discover the design ingenuity of overlooked objects, the Everyday Brilliance of things never destined for more than fleeting relationships with their owners. The amazing world of objects, in other words, made to be used briefly and then thrown away.

Brush With Greatness

Lately, my favorite aisle in the supermarket—after, that is, the one crammed with histrionic cereal boxes—is the orderly section displaying toothbrushes, which stand like sentinels in discreet rows provocatively labeled Soft, Medium, Hard. The tiny toothbrush has become a battleground of innovation and performance, though whether it's actual or merely signified performance is a point of contention. So heated is the showdown between old and new contestants that the shelf space allotted to toothbrush displays has jumped twenty percent to more than four feet in just the past few years.

The toothbrush arena exemplifies just how dynamic the design process has become. Once, a classic, modernist design like Oral B's Indicator, the hard-edged, architectonic brush designed by Braun for Oral B in the late eighties (the two are sister companies owned by Gillette), could dominate the market for over a decade. Now, that lovely translucent brush is about to be "made redundant" (grab some—I'm betting they'll be worth heaps on eBay), to be replaced by the curves, colors, squiggles, and mixed materials familiar to every brush currently screaming "Buy me!" on the shelf. "Toothbrushes are the athletic shoes of our times," says writer Tom

James Wojcik, *coffee cups*, 2000, silver gelatin print, courtesy of James Wojcik

Vanderbilt, "a mature market where manufacturers tout impressive performance claims to eke out advantages in market share and brand equity."

Unlike designers of boutique hotels or bird-encrusted teapots, toothbrush designers are anonymous in their toils. I recently traveled to Frankfurt to talk to Till Winkler, a young designer at Braun who was chosen to create the new Indicator to replace the thirteen-year-old model for Oral B. It was an enlightening exchange:

Q: What's the most difficult challenge about designing a toothbrush?

A: The hardest part is that it looks very simple and it is really difficult. If I tell people I'm a designer of manual toothbrushes and the process takes many months, they think I am crazy.

Q: So what's so hard about it?

A: Perhaps that every detail is very important. You don't think that a toothbrush like this should be very complex but it is.

Q: Is the complexity in the handle or the bristles?

A: It's putting it all together. It starts with the human being because everyone has different hands and you have to make a toothbrush that fits everyone. There are a lot of different ways to use a toothbrush and a toothbrush has to make all the different ways people brush their teeth possible. Just studying their methods is a science.

Q: Is there a risk that Braun could become too trendy with its new design?

A. The original Indicator is a classic, clear, honest design. And people liked it for a long time, and there are still a lot of people who like this design. But now this product looks a little bit old-fashioned. And even when we at Braun say we like it, it's a wonderful product, you can't make it better, it doesn't help us if people aren't buying this product. Management would say, O.K., we'll go to another studio to make the design. We need to sell it.

Q: How will you make a design that sells?

A: Our challenge is that we're looking for new shapes, we're looking for new designs, and we want to try not to forget our roots and to integrate the original honest, classic design into our new products. And that's a very difficult challenge. It's a very small path to find the right way.

The risk represented by not finding its "small path" could cost Oral B a very big share of the toothbrush market. Till Winkler is charged with not just meeting the performance specifications required of a state-of-the-art toothbrush. The object—made to be thrown away after just a few months use—must inspire desire. Enough to make someone reach for it amongst four long feet of highly adorned and very ambitious alternative suitors.

High Stakes Desire

In the case of the Indicator toothbrush, as opposed to, say, the plastic coffee cup lid, designing desire is an expressed requirement, along with engineering, tooling, marketing, and so on. Some companies place a high premium on crafting a design advantage, though surprisingly, most don't. Instead they are led by the empirical forces of engineering, marketing and the bottom line, which dictate the process and outcome of their wares. In the case of the coffee cup lid the design is a pure expression of the object's function; its intrinsic properties convey everything it does. At the opposite extreme is a company like Apple Computer, where design is an obsession and will continue to be as long as Steve Jobs is the Svengali leading the tireless and futile campaign against a monolithic software environment ruled by Windows.

Apple is a company I can adore, not only because it did, as its founder declared, change the world (I really believe this), but also because it is insane about raising the design bar with every new product, year after difficult year. How can one company inspire such unrepentant product lust on such a consistent basis? Because it has to: it's pure survival. Apple computers would not exist without their cult of diehard fans who make considerable trade-offs for innovative breakthroughs in materials, exactingly high tolerances, expressive new forms, and a palpable sense that the product is an intelligent manifestation of what it does. These are no off-the-shelf, one-size-fits-all sheet-metal boxes. And for Apple, it takes sheer fearless passion to go upstream against a river of hard-edge sheet metal.

But despite my unfettered enthusiasm for Apple and a few companies like it, I return to the unsung poetics of anonymous designs. Why do I care so deeply about the humble but stunningly perfect clear plastic PET cup—a clear jewel made to be used once and tossed—and Ben Nicholson's kooky collection of bread ties showcased so provocatively in *Mood River*? Because that's where it all starts. Without these pure, unselfconscious expressions of a problem intuitively well solved, we wouldn't have the antecedents of Apple Computer.

Mood River cast it net wide and reeled in an eclectic, unexpected, *unlikely* collection of artifacts. Significantly, it has made space for the unheralded, anonymous designers at work today. These workaday experts design pens and pencils and plastic cups, toothbrushes, safety helmets, and bike frames with as much care, brilliance, and subtlety as the cover stars of design magazines, yet they and their achievements pass through the world almost unnoticed. If *Mood River* opens a space of recognition for the achievements of the anonymous designer, it does so in the shadow of its stars and superstars. But maybe that's how it should be. After all, isn't the story of Everyday Brilliance really just a version of how each of us master the peculiar particulars of our own lives with our own everyday brilliance, providing the sea of shoulders for those giants to stand on?

Jonathan Ive, Apple's head designer, once told me how a product inspires desire: "It is very difficult to desire something you feel intimidated by," he said. "Once you feel you can understand something, you can truly desire it."

The clear plastic cup and the gleaming white iBook. One is the brilliance of the everyday, the other is brilliance you have to shell out for. Both are heroes in my book.

Chee Pearlman is a design columnist for the New York Times *and a design and editorial consultant for a number of companies and cultural organizations. From 1993 to 2000 she was Editor in Chief of* I.D. Magazine, *which won five National Magazine Awards under her tenure.*

AURORA	AVENGER	BEETLE	BONNEVILLE
CAMRY	CIVIC	CONCORDE	DEVILLE
ESCORT	FIREBIRD	FOCUS ZX3	GRAND AM
PASSAT	PT CRUISER	RIO	RSX

VIPER	3.2 CL	3.2 TL-S	911 CARRERA

BONNEVILE

BOXSTER

BOXSTER

C240

DEVILLE

ECLIPSE

ECLIPSE SPYDER

ELANTRA GLS

GRAND PRIX

GS430

MIATA

MONTE CARLO

SOLARIS

TAURUS

TRIBUTE

V70

top row, left to right:
Oldsmobile AURORA taillight, 2001
Dodge AVENGER taillight, 1998
Volkswagen BEETLE taillight, 2001
Pontiac BONNEVILLE taillight, 2001
Pontiac BONNEVILLE headlight, 2001
Porsche BOXSTER taillight, 2001
Porsche BOXSTER headlight, 2001
Mercedes-Benz C240 headlight, 2002

second row, left to right:
Toyota CAMRY taillight, 2001
Honda CIVIC headlight, 2001
Chrysler CONCORDE taillight, 2001
Cadillac DEVILLE taillight, 2001
Cadillac DEVILLE center taillight, 2001
Mitsubishi ECLIPSE taillight, 2001
Mitsubishi ECLIPSE SPYDER taillight, 1999
Hyundai ELANTRA GLS taillight, 2000

third row, left to right:
Ford ESCORT taillight, 2001
Pontiac FIREBIRD taillight, 2001
Ford FOCUS ZX3 taillight, 2001
Pontiac GRAND AM taillight, 2001
Pontiac GRAND PRIX taillight, 2000
Lexus GS430 taillight, 2001
Mazda MIATA taillight, 2001
Chevrolet MONTE CARLO headlight, 2001

fourth row, left to right:
Volkswagen PASSAT taillight, 2001
Chrysler PT CRUISER taillight, 2001
Kia RIO taillight, 2001
Acura RSX taillight, 2001
Toyota SOLARIS taillight, 2001
Ford TAURUS taillight, 2001
Mazda TRIBUTE headlight, 2001
Volvo V70 taillight, 2001

bottom row, left to right:
Dodge VIPER headlight, 2001
Acura 3.2 CL taillight, 2001
Acura 3.2 TL-S taillight, 2001
Porsche 911 CARRERA taillight, 2001

Courtesy of
Byers Dublin Dodge
Byers Imports on Main
James Gill, Chesrown Oldsmobile
GMC, KIA
Dave Gill Pontiac-GMC
Dennis Mitsubishi Inc
Ed Potter, Inc
Germain Toyota
Immke Crestview Cadillac
Lindsay Acura
MidWestern Auto Group
Nelson Auto Group
Photos: Roman Sapecki

Aquafresh
Colgate
Crest
Fluocaril
Mentadent
Oral-B
Parogencyl
TOOTHBRUSHES
Courtesy of
Colgate Palmolive
The Gillette Company
GlaxoSmithKline
Unilever Home and
Personal Care
Photos: Roman Sapecki

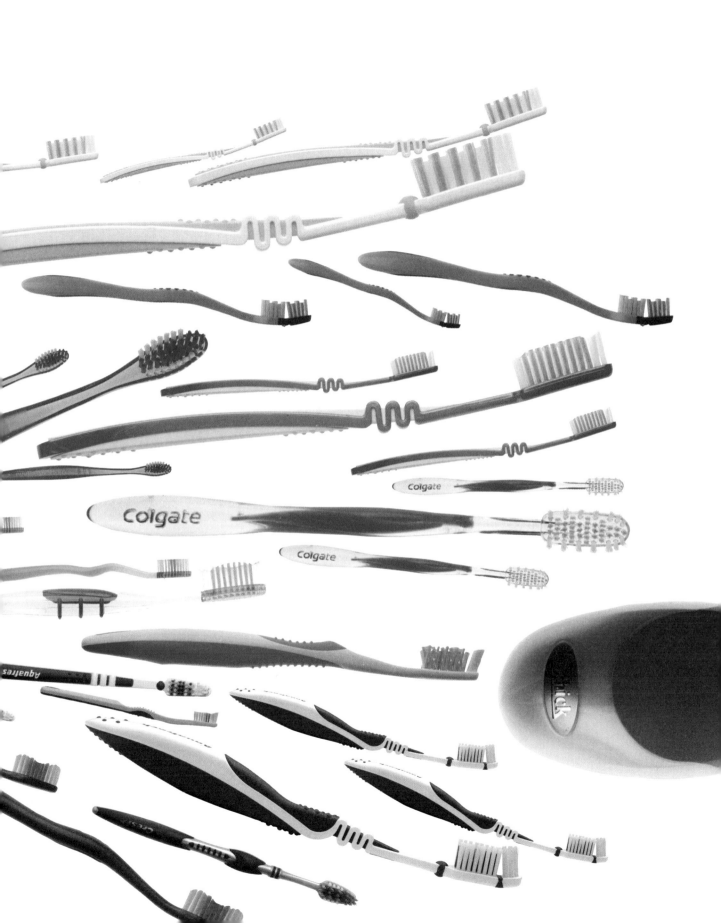

Gillette VENUS
Schick SILK EFFECTS +
Schick PROTECTOR
RAZORS
Courtesy of
The Gillette Company
Pfizer Consumer Group
Photos: Roman Sapecki

MONO CORRECTION TAPE
MONO ADHESIVE
Courtesy of/photos
courtesy of Tombow

Pentel
Pilot
Caran D'Ache
Sensa by Willat
PENS
Courtesy of/photos
courtesy of
Caran D'Ache of
Switzerland
Sensa by Willat
Additional photos:
Roman Sapecki

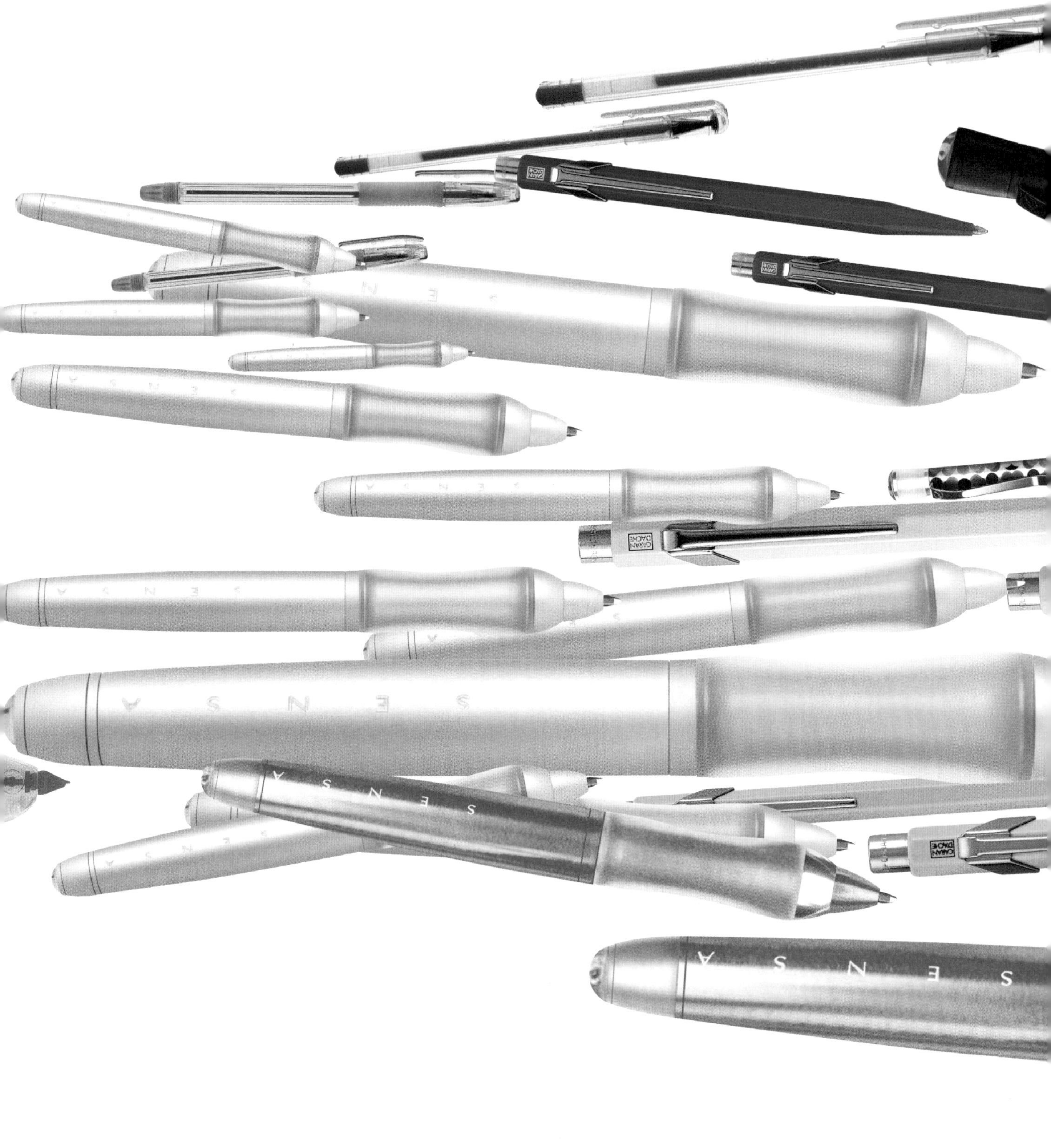

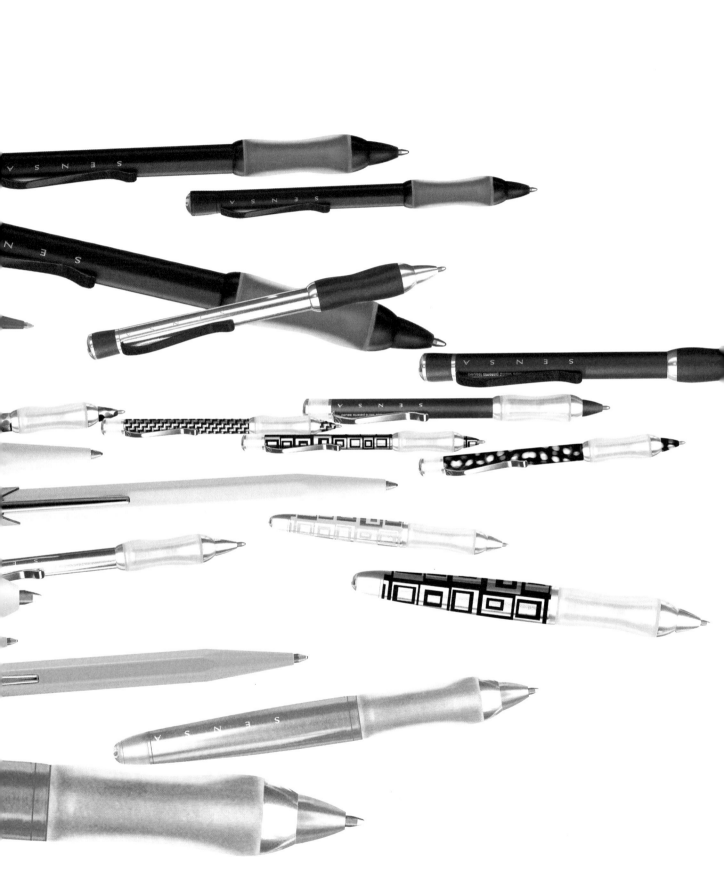

Gillette MACH3
RAZORS
Courtesy of
The Gillette Company

Caran D'Ache
Hold Everything
Kikkerland
Pentech
Sensa by Willat
PENS AND PENCILS
Courtesy of/photos
courtesy of
Caran D'Ache of Switzerland
Sensa by Willat
Additional photos:
Roman Sapecki

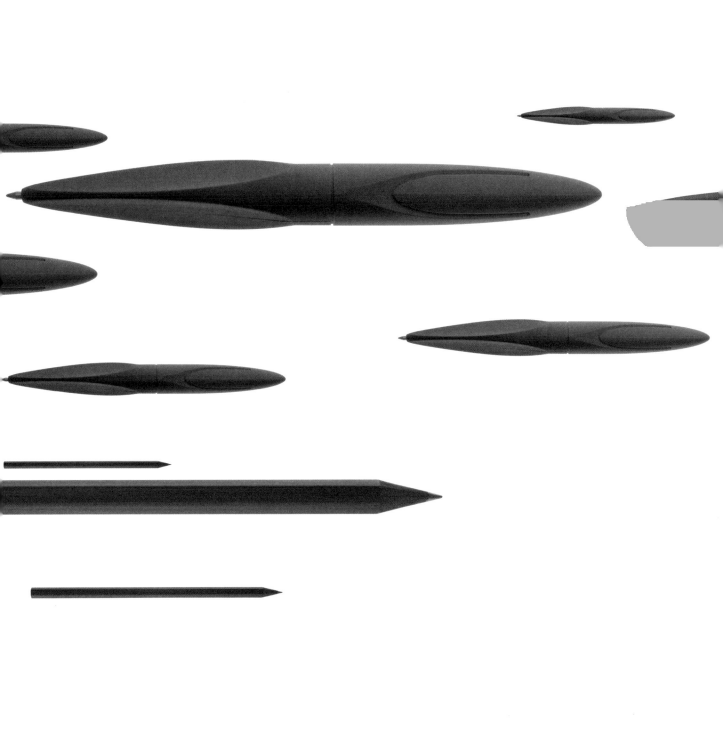

top section, left to right
SLIDING BLADE POWERTOOTH™ PRUNING SAW (#9259)
FISKARS® POWER GEAR BYPASS PRUNER (#7936)
FISKARS® CLASSIC PRO BYPASS PRUNER (#7938)
FISKARS® RATCHET ANVIL PRUNER (#7685)
Courtesy of/photos courtesy of Fiskars Consumer Products, Inc.

STORM LANTERN LIGHTER
Courtesy of AdHoc Entwicklung and Vertrieb GmbH
Photo: Roman Sapecki

CR240DV RECIPROCATING SAW
Courtesy of/photo courtesy of Hitachi Power Tools

DOUBLE GRIP PRUNER
SWISS FELCO PRUNERS (two views)
Courtesy of/photos courtesy of Smith & Hawken

middle section, top to bottom
VITRY PUMICE STONE
Photos: Roman Sapecki

ELIOS ERGOGRIP PEELER
ELIOS JULIENNE PEELER
Courtesy of ISI North America
Photos: Roman Sapecki

bottom row, left to right:
RABBIT CORKSCREW
Designer: Edward Kilduff
Courtesy of/photo courtesy of Metrokane

EURO-PRO SHARK HAND HELD VACUUM
Courtesy of/photo courtesy of Euro-Pro Corporation

OXO GOOD GRIPS SOAP DISPENSING KITCHEN BRUSH
OXO GOOD GRIPS HOUSEHOLD SCRUB BRUSH
Courtesy of/photos courtesy of OXO International

ORANGEX OJEX MANUAL JUICER
Designer: Smart Design, LLC
Courtesy of OrangeX; photo courtesy of
Smart Design, LLC

HEAVY DUTY STAPLE REMOVER
Courtesy of/photo courtesy of Swingline,
a division of ACCO Brands, Inc.

this page, left to right
MIKADO FLATWARE
Designer: Dario Tantoglio
Courtesy of/photo courtesy of Fratelli Guzzini

KOSKINEN 2000
Designer: Harri Koskinen
CITTERIO 2000
Designer: Antonio Citterio
Courtesy of/photos courtesy of Designor Oy/Ab,
Hackman Tools Helsinki, Findland

opposite page, left to right, top to bottom
THE WAVE COLLECTION, 1997
Designer: Will Prindle
Courtesy of/photo courtesy of
Forms+Surfaces

Interdesign USA SQUEEGEE LA RACLOIR
Photo: Roman Sapecki

BIG FOOT RAZOR
Designer: Eric Nanson
Courtesy of Artitudes Designs
Photo courtesy of Eric Nanson

FILIO FRUIT TRAY
Designer: Ralph Krämer
Courtesy of Mono Tabletop
Photo: Roman Sapecki

PREMIUM SPOON REMOVER
Courtesy of/photo courtesy of
Swingline, a division of ACCO Brands, Inc.

FLYSWATTER
Designer: Erik Bagger
Courtesy of/photo courtesy of
Rosendahl A/S, Denmark

BEOCOM 6000
Courtesy of/photo courtesy of
Bang & Olufsen

BABYBOOP
Designer: Ron Arad
Courtesy of/photo courtesy of Museo Alessi

POAA, 1999
Designer: Philippe Starck
Courtesy of xO
Photo: Roman Sapecki

H5010 DOOR LEVER
Designer: Foster and Partners
Courtesy of/photo courtesy of
Valli & Valli USA, Inc.

FILIO FLATWARE
Designer: Ralph Krämer
Courtesy of/photo courtesy of
Mono Tabletop

ZEUG KNIVES
Designer: Michael Schneider
Courtesy of Mono Tabletop
Photo: Roman Sapecki

MERIDIAN DOORPULLS, 2000
Designer: Tom Peters
Courtesy of/photo courtesy of
Forms+Surfaces

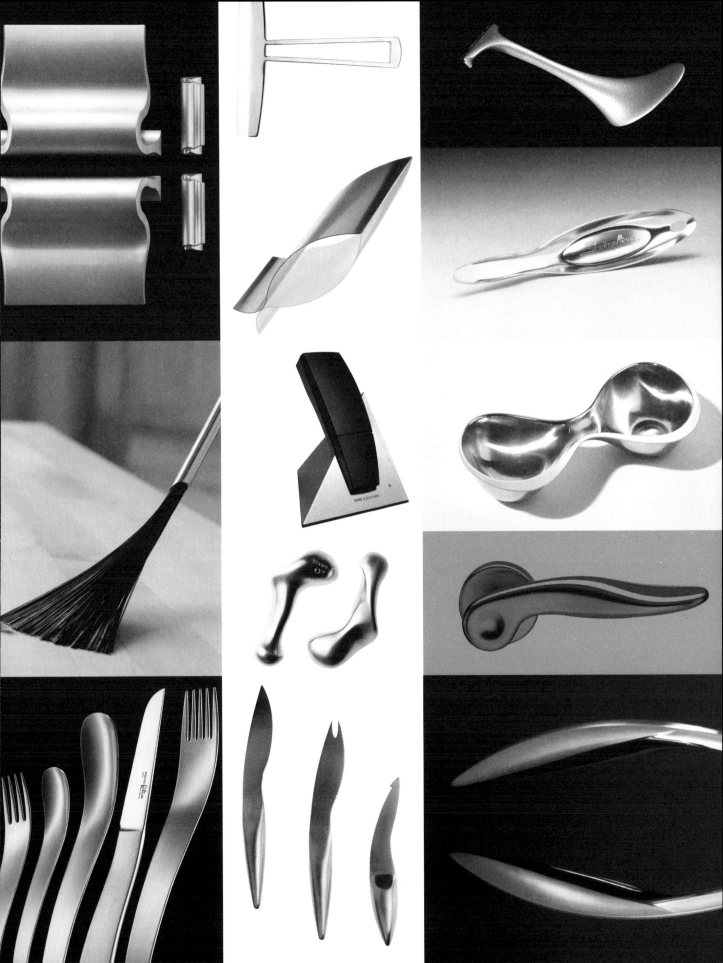

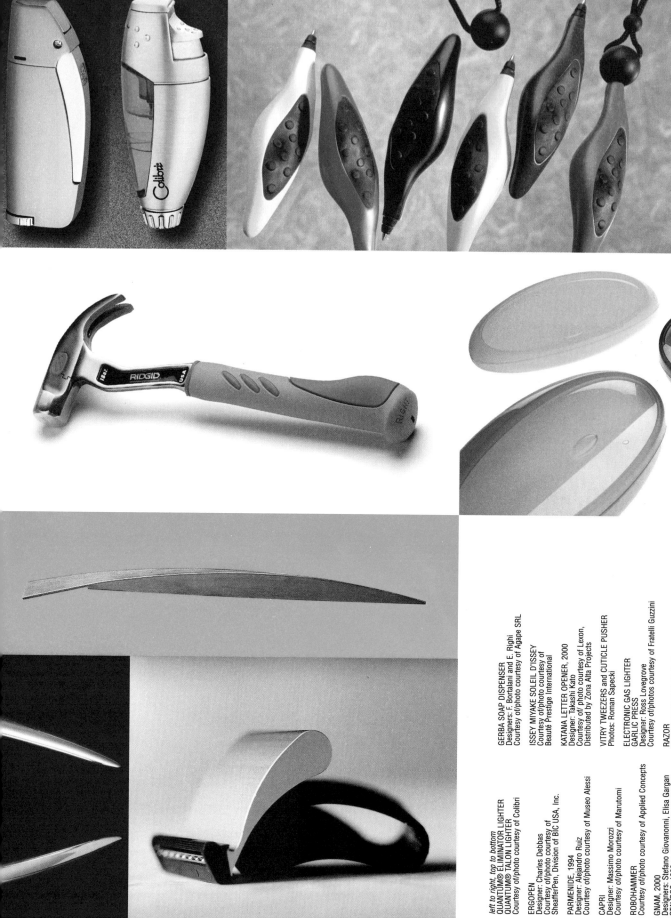

left to right, top to bottom

QUANTUM® ELIMINATOR LIGHTER
QUANTUM® TALON LIGHTER
Courtesy of/photo courtesy of Colibri

ERGOPEN
Designer: Charles Debbas
Courtesy of/photo courtesy of
SheafferPen, Division of BIC USA, Inc.

PARMENIDE, 1994
Designer: Alejandro Ruiz
Courtesy of/photo courtesy of Museo Alessi

CAPRI
Designer: Massimo Morozzi
Courtesy of/photo courtesy of Marutomi

ROBOHAMMER
Courtesy of/photo courtesy of Applied Concepts

GNAM, 2000
Designers: Stefano Giovanonni, Elisa Gargan
STAVROS, 1999
Designer: Marc Newson
Courtesy of/photos courtesy of Museo Alessi

GERBA SOAP DISPENSER
Designers: F. Bortalani and E. Righi
Courtesy of/photo courtesy of Agape SRL

ISSEY MIYAKE SOLEIL D'ISSEY
Courtesy of/photo courtesy of
Beauté Prestige International

KATANA LETTER OPENER, 2000
Designer: Takashi Kato
Courtesy of/ photo courtesy of Lexon,
Distributed by Zona Alta Projects

VITRY TWEEZERS and CUTICLE PUSHER
Photos: Roman Sapecki

ELECTRONIC GAS LIGHTER
GARLIC PRESS
Designer: Ross Lovegrove
Courtesy of/photos courtesy of Fratelli Guzzini

RAZOR
Designer: Flemming Bo Hansen
Courtesy of/photo courtesy of
Rosendahl A/S, Denmark

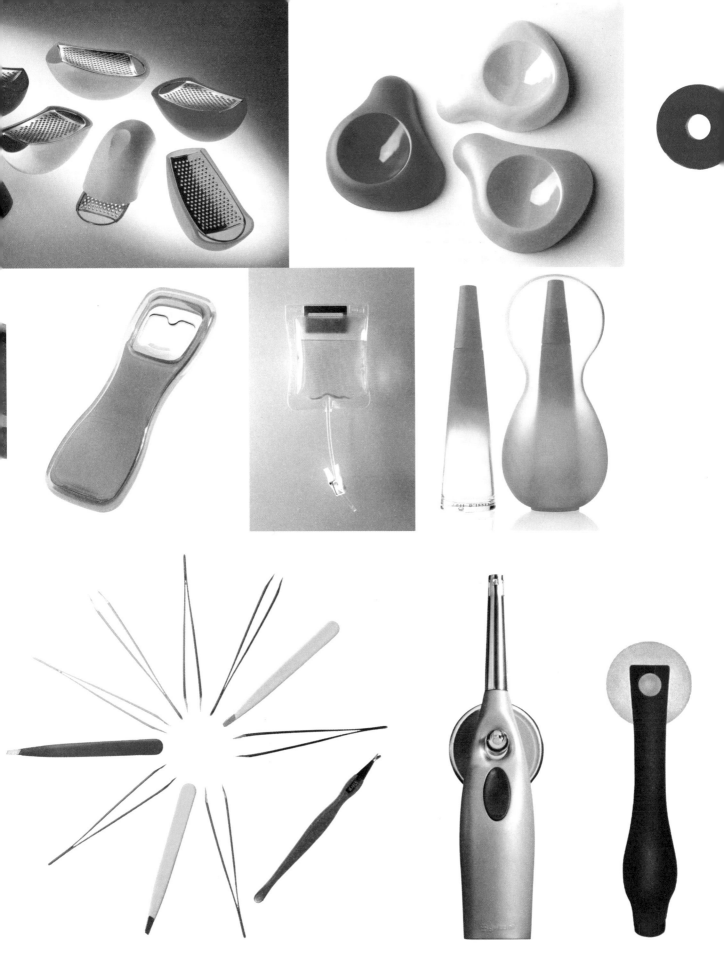

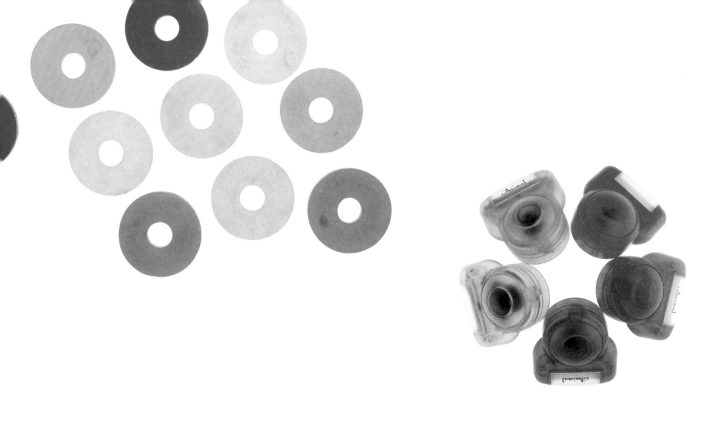
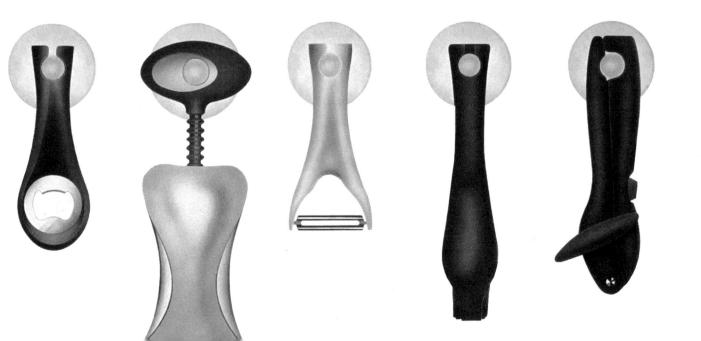

left to right: top to bottom
LIFE SAVERS
Photo: Roman Sapecki

NEON NIGHT LIGHT
Courtesy of Luminair, Inc.
Photo: Roman Sapecki

SMOOTH GRIP DESK STAPLER
TOT GRIP STAPLER
Courtesy of/photos courtesy of
Swingline, a division of
ACCO Brands, Inc.

DC07 DUAL CYCLONE
VACUUM CLEANER
Designer: James Dyson
Courtesy of/photo courtesy of
Dyson, Ltd.

WING FINGER DANCER
Designer: Satoshi Nakagawa
Courtesy of/photo courtesy of
Tripod Design

bottom row, left to right
BOTTLE OPENER
CORKSCREW
POTATO PEELER
NUT CRACKER
CAN OPENER
Designer: Ross Lovegrove
Courtesy of/photos courtesy of
Fratelli Guzzini

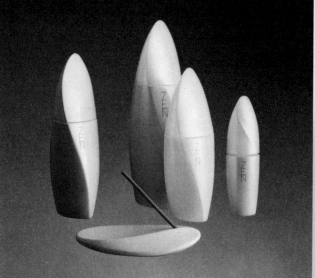

top to bottom, left to right
SAFETY GLIDE
Courtesy of Becton Dickinson
Photo: Roman Sapecki

DC07 DUAL CYCLONE
VACUUM CLEANER
Designer: James Dyson
Courtesy of/photo courtesy of
Dyson, Ltd.

DKNY MEN'S FRAGRANCE
EAU DE TOILETTE
CASHMERE MIST
EAU DE TOILETTE SPRAY
Courtesy of/photos courtesy of
Donna Karan Cosmetics

MUSEUM OF AIRLINE PLASTIC
Courtesy of Chee Pearlman
Photos: Roman Sapecki
(three views)

ZEN
Courtesy of/photo courtesy of
Shiseido, Co.

With almost comic regularity, the history of architecture is marked by repeated moments of reconfiguration.[1] Every time architecture settles down to its supposed business of conserving the status quo, something comes along and demands that it "wake up!" and become again progressive.[2] Thus, today is not the first time that architecture has been challenged by realignments between its social and professional practice and its disciplinary autonomy, by the developments of new technologies and material techniques, and by shifts in the dominant forms of representation. In recent centuries, this constellation of matters—the social, technical, and material stuff of architecture—has been understood as held together not by divine law but by the gravitational pull of modernity, and each orbital realignment has produced modernity anew. Modernity is thus an inconsistent phenomenon, riddled by moments of oscillation that have opened architecture to spaces of significant experimentation and that have demanded extraordinary agility. These ruptures have given to architecture's history dynamic moments of plasticity.

Today, the material and intellectual conditions of architecture are again in a state of flux. While some have responded to this moment of historical plasticity with retrenchment, rigidity, and cynicism, others have found a new optimism in the inventiveness made possible by the plasticizing of architecture. A good, if obvious, example of the generative opportunities of plasticity today is Frank Gehry's *Horse's Head* installation at Gemini Studio. The head is made of molded fiberglass, a plastic material that already began an illustrious history in the reconfiguration of canonic modernism with the work of Charles and Ray Eames. But *la chaise,* for example, is clearly a functional, even anthropomorphic, object while the Gehry head is more radically indeterminate. Moreover, in the *Head,* modern abstraction is so extreme as to exclude even geometry, the regulatory function of lines and of *disegno* has become the supple form of painterliness and color, and the quest for transparency has been enriched by the achievement of luminosity. Each of these adjustments to high modernism is dependent on the plasticity of the material used. But the *Horse's Head* is plastic in a much more significant and architectural way.

This project has a complex etiology: its form was first developed for the Lewis House, then redeployed in the Pariserplatz project in Berlin, redeveloped for an installation at the Gagosian Gallery, and now finds its fourth and probably not last incarnation in the *Horse's Head.* The migration of this evolving form clearly defies the idea that form should follow function and exposes a kind of semi-autonomy in the relation of form and program. Indeed, the project has resisted the moralistic tyranny of program-driven architecture by developing a tactical rather than essentializing attitude toward program and context, and a plastic rather than causal relation between function and form. The very fact that a consistent morphology can serve so many different functions—and not through recourse to the neutrality of the generic—is a demonstration of extreme architectural plasticity. A similar operation using different techniques is Bernard Tschumi's scheme for the African Museum in New York. Unlike the Gehry, Tschumi's project does not rely on plastic as a building material. But the manner in which the building envelope and the interior space are entirely discontinuous similarly eschews the idea of form follows function in favor of the plastic pursuit of program. These examples indicate that plastic is more than the sum of its macromolecules.

This excess plays a very specific if peculiar role in the structure of modern architecture. On the one hand, plastic is everywhere and has provoked a vast array of cultural identifications. We are all always in some form of intimate contact with plastic. It might be in your cavity-prone teeth, in your reconstructed knee, in your pre-saline breast implants, and in the diet chips you ate for lunch. If it's not actually in your body, it's undoubtedly in your clothes, on the upholstery of your chair, in the paint on the walls, and the mechanical systems of the building. The ubiquity of plastic is perhaps best demonstrated by *The Graduate,* directed by Mike Nichols in 1967, where the enormous sense of claustrophobia that is produced through the too many talking heads with bad martini breath crowding around Dustin Hoffman suggests that plastic has taken up so much space that there is no room to breathe—in fact that plastic has swallowed the future itself.

Vilified by plastiphobes and touted as a panacea by plastifiles, plastic is virtually everywhere except in the discipline of architecture. Even though one can barely think modern architecture without thinking materials—the glass house, the brick villa, the steel frame, the concrete city—there is no equivalent plastic typology. Plastic never earned a place in what Jean Baudrillard called the aristocracy of materials; it lacks the essential and immutable qualities that authorized this supposedly natural hierarchy.[3] If glass was the modernist material par excellence, identified with utopia, truth, and lightness, plastic was marked as a product of waste, commodification, and masquerade. Unable to enter the moral logic based on an identity between materials and truth—truth to materials, truth of materials, and so forth—plastic has remained an unethical unmentionable.

When Reyner Banham fell for Roger Vadim's *Barbarella* in 1968, he became more or less the first and only architecture critic to say anything interesting about plastic. In his essay "Triumph of Software" written in 1968, Banham claimed that traditional architecture was giving way to a new form of responsive environment characterized by ambience, and by curved, pliable, continuous, breathing, adaptable surfaces.[4] For Banham, the success of *Barbarella*'s world derived from the fact that it performed like flesh produced through natural materials such as fur and moss or their artificial equivalents: inflated, transparent plastic membranes.

But Banham's opposition between hardware and software, between the traditional city of modernism and the plastic environment of the future too easily saw plastic simply as a new technological means to further modernist ends. In contrast, precisely because of its lack of ethical and formal restrictions, plastic uncovers the material unconscious of a neglected modernity that resists the ideology of high modernism by occupying a position somewhere between culture and matter. *Barbarella*'s plastic artificial world is not opposed to the nature that authorized the Renaissance vision with which it has been compared but stealthily just assumes its place; the ocean from which Venus emerges becomes in *Barbarella* the erotic plastic landscape of the chamber of dreams. Ultimately, this substitution deforms modernism's idealized representations. When Jane Fonda is entrapped by gravity she is oddly disfigured by the perfect transparency of her plastic bed. In fact, it is modernity itself that is disfigured by a plastic already embedded within modernity's ideology.

There are certain irreducible aspects of plastic as a category of material that are incommensurable with the logic of modernism: plastic is a synthetic liquid material in a state of arrest. The combination of artificiality and instability defies the essentializing and naturalizing of materials that were central to modernist discourse. If brick had such an unchanging and reliable nature that it could consistently tell you what it wanted to be, plastic does not adhere to any such universal grammar or authorize a material discipline.

Plasticity as an ideology and an adjective, however, is distinct from plastic as a material and a noun. The actual invention of plastics in the molecular sense took place only during the nine-

teenth century. The ideological role of plasticity in the arts, however, is as old as architectural discourse itself and begins with Vitruvius. His *Ten Books* are the first to have codified the term the plastic arts, one of many terms he took from the Greek, in this case from the term *plassein,* or to mold. Vitruvius defined the plastic arts in relation to the molding process required in their production. Ceramics, stucco, and plasters, even sculpture, were characterized for Vitruvius by their plasticity. This rootedness in material and manual labor is what made the plastic arts also the lesser arts. In contrast, Vitruvius defined the liberal arts in relation to abstract rather than formal or material properties. The liberal arts originated not in a process of manufacture but in ideas produced in the mind of the artist and thus were accorded a much higher cultural status. Most importantly, the liberal arts were those that signified via imitation, narrative, and so forth while the plastic arts were those that were made in a particularly fluid way. Thus, by the turn of the twentieth century, when Le Corbusier defined architecture as a plastic thing, "chose de plastique," as a pure creation of the mind that called not for the architect but for "le plasticien," he was referring to an antique ideology of form making rather than to a synthetic polymer or a vanguard rhetoric of modern industrial materials.[5]

Although this fact has never been noted, almost every major modern architect from Frank Lloyd Wright to Le Corbusier, from Hannes Meyer to Richard Neutra was interested in this kind of plasticity and claimed it as a defining and privileged feature of modernism itself. To take just one example, Wright wrote his famous essay "In the Nature of Materials" in 1943, long before plastic had become a significant factor in building construction: he himself had primary contact with plastic in the form of silicon used in building with glass. Nevertheless, Wright claimed in this essay that plastic "is peculiarly modern." "Plasticity" for Wright is nothing less than "the true aesthetic of genuine structural reality."[6] Unlike glass and steel, to which Wright assigns essential characteristics, plastic is a material without a nature but plasticity is a concept with an aesthetic. Plastic hence both structures modernity—it is modernity for Wright and Le Corbusier in the form of plasticity—and plastic exceeds modernity's logic when in the form of a material without an ethical mandate. Plastic has thus troubled the Vitruvian classification of the arts, by suggesting that architecture could both be plastic, defined in relation to its mode of production, and characterized by plasticity in relation to its mode of signification. Occupying the very space

of this contradiction between the will to signify and will to be formed, architecture has always been especially haunted by this disciplinary plasticity.

Never more so than during the 1960s when the idea of plasticity complexly converged with an intense architectural interest in the new materials of plastics. It was at that moment that plastic did its most energetic work in undoing modernism's authority and began to exploit the flexible structure of architecture's discipli-

The Cushicle   Mike Webb

The Cushicle is an invention that enables a man to carry a complete environment on his back. It inflates-out when needed. It is a complete nomadic unit – and it is fully serviced.

It enables an explorer, wanderer or other itinerant to have a high standard of comfort with a minimum effort.

The illustrations show the two main parts of the Cushicle unit as they expand out from their unpacked state to the domestic condition. One constituent part is the 'armature' or 'spinal' system. This forms the chassis and support for the appliances and other apparatus. The other major element is the enclosure part which is basically an inflated envelope with extra skins as viewing screens. Both systems open out consecutively or can be used independently.

The Cushicle carries food, water supply, radio, miniature projection television and heating apparatus. The radio, TV, etc., are contained in the helmet and the food and water supply are carried in pod attachments.

With the establishment of service nodes and additional optional apparatus, the autonomous Cushicle unit could develop to become part of a more widespread urban system of personalized enclosures.

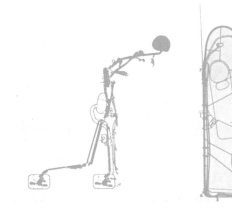

Stage 1
chassis unopened

Stage 2
suit unopened

Cushicle 1966–7 Michael Webb

Stage 5
combination opening out further

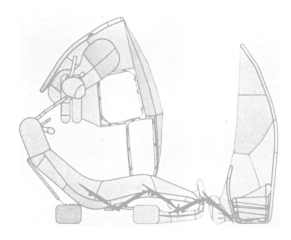

64

nary instability. Three projects of the 1960s can be used to explore this phenomenon: Claes Oldenburg's *Bedroom Ensemble* of 1963–69, Michael Webb's *Cushicle* of 1966–67 and Joe Colombo's *Total Furnishing Unit* of 1969–72. Each of these projects uses plastic in formally different ways: Oldenburg as a kind of industrial canvas, Webb as a skin, and Colombo as a semisolid block. All were considered prototypes primarily for exhibition purposes and all share a domestic program. From an architectural point of view, they are relatively minor projects, a choice necessitated by the fact that plastic has been kept out not only of the nobility of materials but of the nobility of the canon—it is still hard to conceive of an architectural monument made of plastic. While they differ significantly in cultural context and in their configuration of domesticity, in formal character and in their deployment of plastic, they all use techniques of plasticity to interpose gaps into modern orthodoxies.

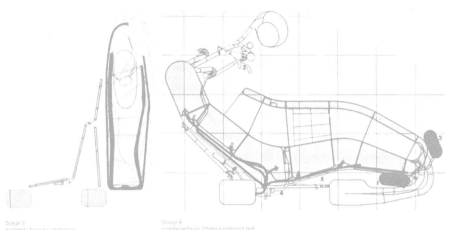

Stage 3
suit and chassis climbing

Stage 4
combined suit, chassis opening out

Stage 6
total Cushicle fully opened out and in use

Stages 1–6, as illustrated in *Archigram* (1973)

Oldenburg's *Bedroom Ensemble* was first installed in 1963 in the front room of the Sidney Janis Gallery for an exhibition entitled "Four Environments" held in 1964 in New York.[7] Conceived while Oldenburg was living in Los Angeles and experimenting extensively with various techniques of using plastic, from vacuum forming to inflatables, the project refers to a motel on the Pacific Coast Highway where every room was decorated with a different animal

pattern: the zebra room, the leopard room etc. One might say that Oldenburg domesticated this artificial zoo by a process of plastification. The project focuses on what Oldenburg described as the "softest room in the house."[8] It is an immediate prelude to the better-known work often called "Softies," a series of partially inflated and thus dysfunctional, plastic domestic consumer objects. Like the Softies, this psychologically soft room is entirely covered in and partially made of plastic, with the surfaces treated such that every conceivable natural or at least traditional material is imitated—false fur skins abound, marbleized Formica covers the tables, the bed is covered in leatherette, and the faux Pollocks were made of printed cloth. *Bedroom* uses plastic both actually and virtually: while in one respect all the surfaces imitate other materials and thus exploit plastic's capacity for masquerade, as the sheen of the toilet mimics ceramic, the imitation in *Bedroom* is always incomplete: the silkscreened fur is left flat and smooth, the marbles are in the wrong colors, etc. Thus, the surfaces refer both to their role in simulation and to the characteristics of colorability and smoothness that were particularly associated with plastic.

But unlike the Softies, the *Bedroom Ensemble* is deliberately hard. The dripping solids of the Softies suggest a state somewhere between painting and sculpture, but the hardness of *Bedroom Ensemble* was clearly meant to suggest architecture. Oldenburg wrote, "*Bedroom* might have been called composition for (rhomboids) columns and disks."[9] Not only was Oldenburg particularly interested in geometry, which he associated with architecture, but this is the first of Oldenburg's projects to require what is called the technical style of drawing and model making that approximates the architectural construction or working document. Every detail was worked out in relation to the existing architectural conditions, and he conceived of the process of construction in architectural, indeed Albertian, terms: an "object made by conventional industrial procedure according to plans by the artist serving his purposes."[10] As Oldenburg's work entered the sphere of the domestic, into the "nature of materials" and into industrialized modes of production, it seems to have acquired the need for an architectural armature.

But *Bedroom Ensemble* is not traditionally architectural. First of all, there is no room here for inhabitation. *Bedroom Ensemble* may be located in the softest room in the home, yet it is harshly uninviting. The viewer doesn't want to live here, nor can you live

65

in this space lost between the motel and the gallery, nor does anyone live in this temporary and virtual space, clearly marked private with the female subject of the leopard skin coat somehow long gone. *Bedroom Ensemble* is architectural not functionally but rather insofar as it occupies a position between the plastic and the liberal arts, between a mode of production and a mode of signification. *Bedroom Ensemble*, moreover, produces a realm between these two and three dimensions and exhibits what one might call dimensional plasticity. The installation is constructed as though it were a perspective drawing, built in a trapezoidal shape with hard edges used to produce the converging lines of a vanishing point. Oldenburg described his work on the *Ensemble* as "upholstering perspective," which transformed "the rationalization of sight" into a physical fact.[11] The project is, in other words, plastic not simply because of the materials used in its construction. More significant is its treatment of the visual field as a molded and constructed form of material, not as pure projection. *Bedroom Ensemble* becomes architecture exactly at the moment that it defines itself in relation to both sets of Vitruvian terms: it molds the image and is thus a plastic art but represents an image and is thus a liberal art.

If *Bedroom* manipulates weaknesses in representational stability to shape for architecture a form of disciplinary plasticity, Archigram performed similar mutations through a kind of technological dissociation. Invoking the operations of disposability, designed obsolescence, and nomadic impermanence, the *Cushicle* produces the plasticity of indeterminacy. The *Cushicle* is a media-saturated mobile home, a plastic inflatable suit attached to an automotive chassis that permits one to be plugged in and on the move at all times. Designed to be carried by a man on his back, the plastic skins unfold in various configurations creating at once enclosure, media screens, and appliance armatures. A complex prosthetic device, the *Cushicle* is simultaneously subject and object: when closed, with its spine, head, and skin, its seems to be the robotic subject of this itinerant domestic device but when fully opened the robot who seemed to live in the house becomes the house itself. No other subject seems to be required to watch what is on television in this media architecture: the house watches the screens and goes for a ride in the *Cushicle*.[12]

Cushicle engages few of the representational issues raised by Oldenburg's *Bedroom*. Instead, it is better understood in relation to the failed attempts to ennoble plastic and to embrace it within a

properly defined material peerage. This effort to stabilize the ethical and class structure of materials required arguing that plastic was like other material, only better.[13] This of course backfired and plastic became characterized not in terms of Wright's notion of aesthetic and structural continuity or Le Corbusier's ideas about plastic emotions, but in terms of representational imposture. Formica in particular would come to threaten the logical difference between surface and depth, structure and artifice, emerging as a Faustian material that could look like anything and could thus transform all materials into so many arbitrary links in the chain of cultural signification.[14]

This need to find for plastic what Eero Saarinen called "a proper place in architecture" raised tremendous anxiety, even for Charles Eames with whom one associates significant plastic production.[15] Saarinen embraced the fully plastic chair, for example in his pedestal chair, but Eames considered plastic a spineless material that offered no resistance. He claimed that you could make terrible mistakes in plastic and felt that its use should be reserved for artists over fifty.[16] Eames was right to try to use plastic as a repository for anxiety about impending old age and developing youth culture, because plastics were in fact becoming the home of the future. In the Monsanto House by Hamilton and Goody and the Smithsons' House of the Future, both of 1957, the continuity of

material surfaces, moving from structure to furniture to appliances, enmeshed the architecture with its various prosthetics. Unlike Le Corbusier's notion of equipment, which the Smithsons believed kept equipment hierarchically subservient to the architectural envelope, the molded plastic shells of these houses of the future appear as residual byproducts of the organization of appliances. The plastic arts generate the architecture rather than lie subservient to it in direct contradiction to the Vitruvian hierarchy. The *Cushicle* relates thus more to this operational aspect of the Smithsons' Appliance House, which was completely covered in white Formica, than to Oldenburg's insistently exhibitionist focus on the representational falsity of the plastic surface in *Bedroom*. In the hands of Archigram, plastic suggests an architectural epidermis pushed and pulled by the organs of domestic technology.

The softness of these inflatable membranes likened by Banham to human skin rely on the way plastic was becoming a new form of natural tissue. But the soft plasticity of Archigram's bubbles also plays much more specific and strategic architectural roles. The use of foldable, pliable maneuverable plastic surfaces permitted the betrayal of architectural categories. In the *Living 1990* exhibition done by the whole Archigram group in 1967, for example, floors become furniture, furniture becomes walls, walls disgorge robots, and all depend on the variable softness permitted by plastic materials. This architectural defiance contrasts sharply to other equally skin-like plastic projects of the era. For example, at the 1964 New York World's Fair, many of the corporate pavilions were built of plastic skins. Perhaps most notable among them is Saarinen's IBM pavilion, which contained one of the Eames' multiscreen projects inside. The pavilion was criticized for not being architectural. Instead, it was called environmental, because it allowed for an unregulated flow of visitors and events below. Saarinen's use of plastic was essential to this perception since it was plastic that suggested the mutation of architecture into a new nature developing the organic vocabulary of skins and environments that so captivated Banham.[17]

The *Cushicle* explored this equivocally architectural status even further. The device was one of a series of Archigram projects conceived as gizmos and gadgets rather than buildings, such as the *Living Pod* by David Greene of 1968 or Webb's *Suitaloon*, a totally personalized environment that could plug into either a *Cushicle* for mobility or another *Suit*. The *Cushicle* is not a building but is simultaneously screen and projection device, immersive image and theater space, spectator and spectacle. The observer has no unified image to see, the skin is broken into disjunctive pieces and the observer is not only immersed in the image but is simultaneously caught in the apparatus and technologies of visuality. As the group said about the *LIVING City* project, it "takes the form of a complete structure [and] an organism designed to condition the spectator by cutting him off from the everyday situation, where things are seen in predictable and accepted relationships."[18] In this sense, the *Cushicle* plastically defies both technical and disciplinary distinctions between modes of production and modes of representation.

The programmatic and geographical fluidity of these projects, the elastic and cartoonlike quality of the drawings, and the treatment of these units as so many disposable consumer commodities lent to the parameters of architecture considerable instability. In fact, when *Cushicle* was published in *Archigram* 8,

the editorial text clearly states "we have no buildings here."[19] Instead, what they had was plastic shifting between being a kind of material and a form of behavior. Plastic is thus not hardware or software, terms Archigram introduced in the same issue of their publication as the *Cushicle*, but the indeterminate third term between what they described as tangible, touchable objects and programmatic systems that can be transmitted but not touched. The combination of plastic and plasticity, for Archigram, produced a form of indeterminacy that the group asserted "threatened the propriety of architectural values," not because it was immoral but because it was amoral.[20]

If *Bedroom Ensemble* and *Cushicle* acted to plasticize architecture through representational and technical means, Joe Colombo's *Total Furnishing Unit* designed for the Museum of Modern Art exhibition titled *Italy: The New Domestic Landscape,* used formal and programmatic conditions of homogeneity to similar ends.[21] During the early 1960s, Colombo worked systematically on standalone pieces of furniture and domestic appurtenances, including the *Universale* chair of 1965 and the *Boby* of 1970. Gradually, however, this emphasis on the design of individual objects gave way to increasingly complex and ultimately self-contained environments. Thus Colombo began with furniture, which became equipment, which became multifunctional appliances that deal with environments, especially domestic modular units, and that finally became the *Total Furnishing Unit*, one of the last projects he did before he died.[22]

Although this increased emphasis on environments and programs would seem to suggest an increased alignment with architecture, the reverse is true. Colombo published an outright assault on architecture entitled "Antidesign."[23] For Colombo, the hierarchical subordination of furniture to architecture reinforced the separation of modes of production from design and produced a "confused and disordered habitat filled with a bazaar of disparate objects." In other words, the cult of the object was the result of architecture's claim to be a spatial art that relegated all else to some lower and uncoordinated status—that tried to position architecture as a liberal art by distancing itself from the plastic arts. Colombo suggested instead that one begin with the design of the plastic object that produces the space immediately containing the space of living. The result was a kind of ergonomic design that strove to eliminate conventional architecture altogether. The *Total Furnishing Unit* contains all the necessary requirements, spatial, programmatic, and technical, of the modern house, but it lacks the house itself.

Plastic was, for Colombo, the key to this dispossession of architecture for it alone provided the means needed to eliminate the disciplinary hierarchies on which architecture had thrived. Colombo defined homogeneity as the basic premise underlying his designs, and indeed the individual components of the *Total Furnishing Unit* are deployed with such density that they suggest almost a homogenous mass squeezing out any functional space except the basic ergonomic envelope of the body. But more than just their density produces this effect: the almost seamless surfaces of their thermoset plastic repress any indication of joinery and disconnection. Furthermore, while Oldenburg and Webb relied on distinctions between surface and depth, between skin and structure, Colombo's house is almost an uninterrupted piece of plastic, a smooth and semisolid zone perforated only by the movements of domestic activity.

Modern architects of the 1920s and 1930s eliminated things like moldings and sculptural treatment from the surfaces of their walls in order to keep dust and other detritus from sticking. In other words, they mobilized a certain notion of hygiene in order to cleanse architecture from its contact with the plastic arts. Colombo, in contrast, totally smothered architecture in plastic, seemingly absorbing the discipline itself into this macromolecular structure. In describing a similar project for the same exhibition, Ettore Sottsass said "it is a kind of orgy of the use of plastic, regarded as a material that allows an almost complete process of deconditioning from the interminable chain of psycho-erotic self indulgences about 'possession.'... Ultimately, we feel so detached, so disinterested, and so uninvolved that... after a time it fades away and disappears."[24] The smooth, jointless, textureless surfaces of Colombo's plastic resist all attachment whether in the form of dirt or psychological projection and especially resist the stabilities of architecture.

When a few years after the *New Domestic Landscape* exhibition Colin Rowe, writing about the New York 5, used the term "plastic" to describe the physique side of the physique-flesh, morale-word antithesis, he was exactly restoring the kind of opposition that plasticity was working to undermine.[25] Moreover, Rowe's consistent emphasis on the narrowly architectural belies a different aspect of the work of the 1960s that is important again today, namely the relation of architecture to the plastic and traditionally lesser arts. Just as many of the great designers of plastics began as architects, such as Colombo, Sottsass, and Anna Castelli Ferrieri, architecture today is fundamentally unthinkable without its relation to decorative arts, industrial design, and fashion. Plastic, moreover, is where all of these cultural practices collide. Rem Koolhaas's work for Prada, for example, relies on plastic as the material and conceptual matrix for cultural and psychological plasticity. When $500 shoes are more noteworthy for their plastic soles than for their leather uppers, one can feel the release from the opposition of real and fake and from what Anna Castelli described as its "ambiguous association with political protest."[26] Plastic clothes, plastic displays, programmatic plasticity, plastic money, and social plasticity encourage a new kind of disequilibrium: as you shop yourself into an orgy of Prada plastic, even you can mutate into a new form.

If plasticity is now permitting architecture to be reinvigorated rather than tainted by contact with the decorative arts, it is also permitting a new interest in decoration itself to emerge. While both the Gehry *Horse's Head* and the Herzog and de Meuron Ricola Headquarters are materially plastic, for example, they demonstrate the agility of a plastic decoration that can work through form as well as surface and texture: the *Head* could be called decorative while the box is decorated and both use plasticity to stretch and enfold the moral certainties of such terms. The projects, moreover, demonstrate the fluid intermingling of architecture with graphic design on the one hand and landscape design at the other extreme where a photographic impression, in the case of Herzog and de Meuron, and a flow, in the case of Gehry, mold a new sensibility. Most importantly, if one of the primary definitions of decoration is that which exceeds, that which constitutes surplus beyond necessary structure, both projects are fully excessive. But in neither case can the excess be excised for without the superfluity of plastic there are no projects here.

With these descriptions we are back to how plastic operates to dislodge the very disciplinary structure of architecture. In addition to questions of program, decoration, and the relation between media, perhaps one of the most important issues raised by the plasticity of the contemporary moment involves a radical reorientation in the notion of architectural space. Rather than an empty abstraction, the plastic diagram of space describes a gradual differentiation of material densities ranging from the invisibility of a gas, to a translucent liquid, to a solid form. Diller and Scofidio's Blur Building, for example, transforms glass into a kind of opacity where sight and space are overcome by the liquid plasticity of the solidifying atmosphere. This capacity to produce these spatial and optical effects of plastic without any reliance on the material itself is one of contemporary architecture's most interesting developments. In Preston Scott Cohen's competition scheme for Eyebeam Atelier, for example, the material, formal, disciplinary, and experiential promiscuously mingle to produce a kind of environmental elixir.

As demonstrated by this array of diverse projects, plasticity today obeys no conventional formal or semiological logic and instead exploits gaps in the discipline's stabilities to produce experimental sensibilities. Indeed, for Roberto Unger, plasticity is that which works against those structures that "imprison experiments... within... authoritative ideals," of which the discipline of architecture is a prime example.[27] Instead, plasticity suggests an architectural behavior that works toward an ecology of recombinant productivity. Its efficacy derives, first, from the fact that not only does plastic lack traditional material ethics but also from the fact that plasticity is an unsettling diagram of the negotiation between concept and materiality. Second, plasticity both constitutes and exceeds the modern, its fluid agility embodying an aim that modernity's obsession with structural and formal regulation repressed. Today, most significantly, plastic's double status as a desire to be made and molded, as well as a desire to signify, is producing a multivalent sensibility in which the clarity of view at the core of the Enlightenment project gives way to the density of experience. Meaningful without signification, progressive but not avant-garde, formed but without abjection, architectural but without hierarchy, plasticity is at the core of the contemporary architectural project.

Sylvia Lavin is Chair of the Department of Architecture and Urban Design at UCLA. She is the author of Quatremère de Quincy and the Invention of a Modern Language of Architecture *(MIT) and a forthcoming book on Richard Neutra.*

1 I first explored the material of this essay in the context of a graduate seminar conducted with students at UCLA. I would like to thank them for their lively participation.

2 Moved by the events of September 11, 2001, Herbert Muschamp published such a call to awakening in the *New York Times,* Sunday, October 1, 2001.

3 Jean Baudrillard, "Natural Wood, Cultural Wood," reprinted in *The Plastics Age: From Bakelite to Beanbags and Beyond*, ed. Penny Sparke (New York, 1993).

4 Reyner Bahnham, "Triumph of Software," in *Reyner Banham: Design By Choice*, ed. Penny Sparke (New York, 1981).

5 Le Corbusier, *Vers une Architecture* (Paris, 1928), xx and xix.

6 Frank Lloyd Wright, "In the Nature of Materials: A Philosophy," reprinted in *Architecture Culture, 1943–68,* ed. Joan Ockman (New York, 1993), 35.

7 Oldenburg rebuilt *Bedroom Ensemble* for the Pop Art exhibition at the Hayward Gallery, London, in 1969 and again later that year in his retrospective at the Museum of Modern Art, New York.

8 Cited in Barbara Rose, *Claes Oldenburg* (New York, 1970), 193. *Bedroom Ensemble* is often used to mark Oldenburg's shift in attention away from the life of the street and into the home.

9 Cited in Barbara Rose, *Claes Oldenburg.*

10 Claes Oldenburg, *The Mouse Museum: The Ray Gun Wing* (Cologne, 1979), 55.

11 Cited in Rose, *Claes Oldenburg.*

12 *Cuschicle* was included in *Archigram* 8, ed. Peter Cook, London, 1968.

13 See the 1947 issue of *House Beautiful* entirely devoted to plastics.

14 See Ezio Manzini, *The Material of Invention* (Milan, 1986).

15 Eero Saarinen, "On Architecture," in *Saarinen on His Work* (New Haven, Connecticut, 1962).

16 Cited in Stephen Fenichell, *Plastic: The Making of a Synthetic Century* (New York, 1996).

17 On the 1964 World's Fair, see *Remembering the Future: The New York World's Fair from 1939 to 1964* (New York, 1989).

18 See "Living City," in *Archigram*, ed. Peter Cook (New York, 1999), 20.

19 See *Archigram* 8, unpaginated.

20 See *Archigram* 8, unpaginated.

21 *Italy: The New Domestic Landscape*, ed. Emilio Ambasz (New York, 1972).

22 For a general overview of Colombo's work, see *I Colombo*, ed. V. Fagone (Milan, 1995).

23 First published in *Casabella* in 1969, the essay is reprinted in *I Colombo*, 219. The essay is often misunderstood as a guilt-ridden attack on the fetishistic attachment to consumer objects created in large measure due to the seductive allure of Colombo's own products.

24 *Italy: The New Domestic Landscape*, 162.

25 Colin Rowe, "Introduction," *Five Architects* (New York, 1975).

26 See Anna Castelli Ferrieri in *Plastics + Design*, ed. Renate Ulmer et al (Munich 1997), unpaginated insert.

27 See Roberto Unger, *Plasticty into Power* (Cambridge and New York, 1987), 12 and 206–08.

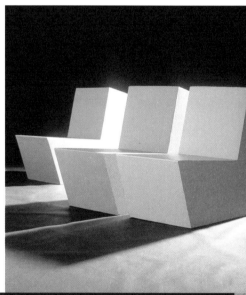

top
SOLO
Designers: Quinze & Milan
Courtesy of /photo courtesy of VISA VERSA

left to right
LOUNGE
Designers: Quinze & Milan
Courtesy of /photo courtesy of VISA VERSA

HP01 TAFEL ALU
Designer: Hans de Pelsmacker
Photo courtesy of E15

POLAR CHAIR
Designer: Matthew Butler
Courtesy of/photo courtesy of Bluesquare

Z
Designer: Giovanni Pagnotta
Courtesy of/photo courtesy of Giovanni Pagnotta

LCP SPRING CHAIR
Designer: Martin van Severen
Courtesy of/photo courtesy of Kartell

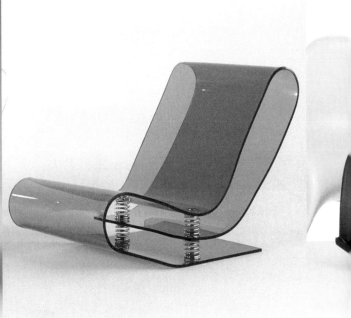

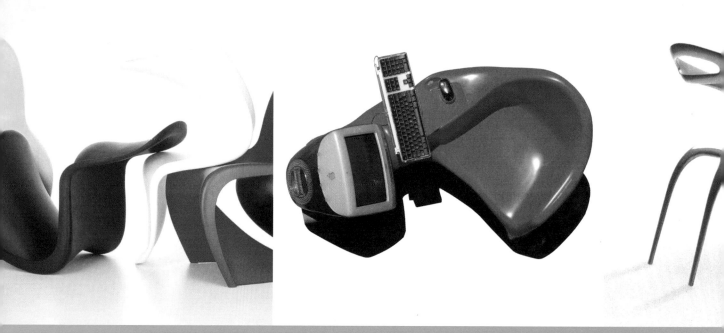

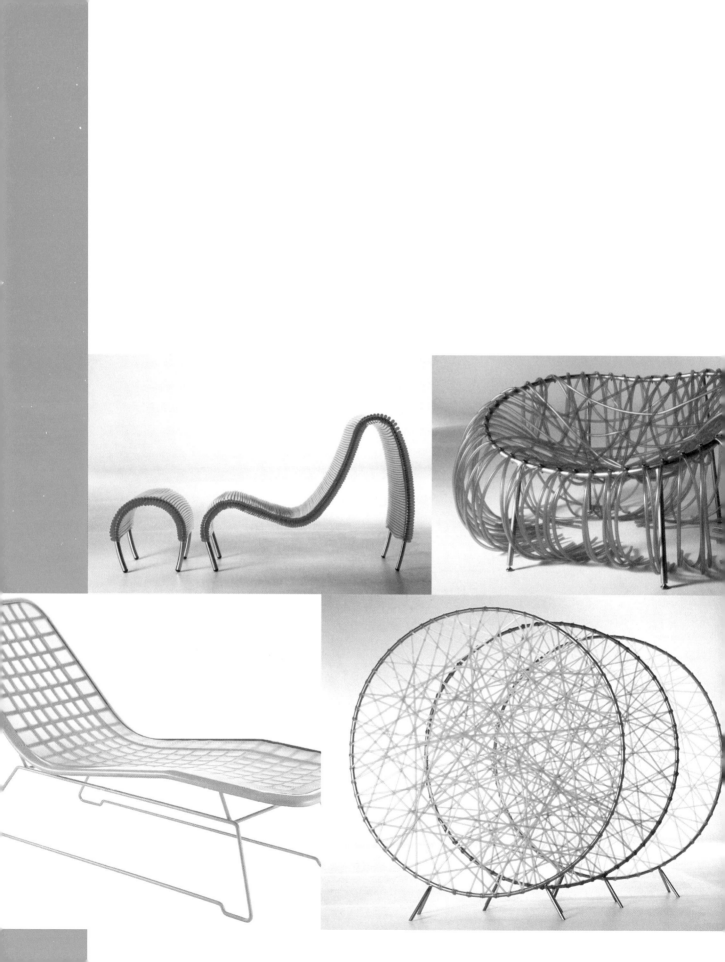

top row, left to right
PORÓROCA, 2001
Designer: Flavia Alves de Souza
Courtesy of/photo courtesy of Edra Spa

ANEMONE CHAIR
Designers: Fernando and Humberto Campana
Courtesy of/photo courtesy of Edra Spa

bottom row, left to right
SOFT, 1999
Designer: Werner Aisslinger
Photo courtesy of Zanotta Spa

ZIG ZAG PARAVENTO SCREEN, 2001
Designers: Fernando and Humberto Campana
Courtesy of/photo courtesy of Edra Spa

CHAIR #1, 2001
Designer: Ansel Thompson
Courtesy of/photo courtesy of Ansel Thompson

EXTRATERRAIN
Designer: Kivi Sotamaa
Courtesy of Kivi Sotamaa and Markus Holmsten
Photo: Petrivirtanen, Central Art Archives, Helsinki

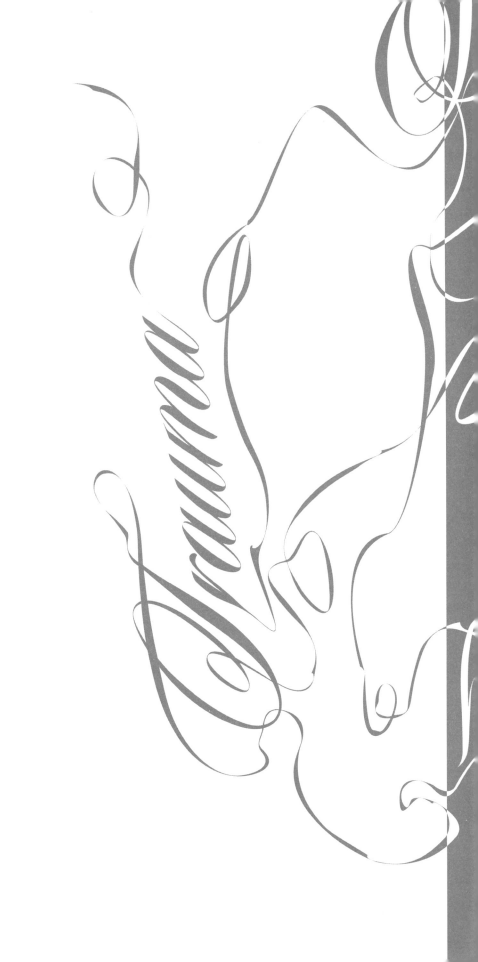

left to right
FRAGILE
Designer: Ben Van Berkel
Photo courtesy of Cor Unum

STEALTH FIGHTER
Photo: Denny Lombard, courtesy of
Lockheed Martin Aeronautics Company

CHURCH OF THE YEAR 2000
Designer: Peter Eisenman
Courtesy of/photo courtesy of
Canadian Centre for Architecture

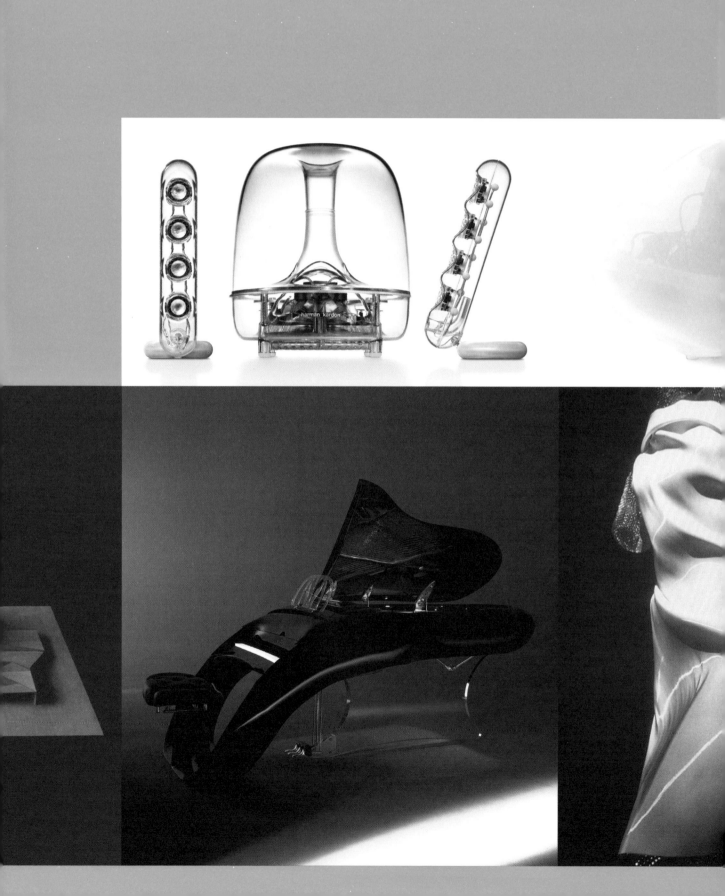

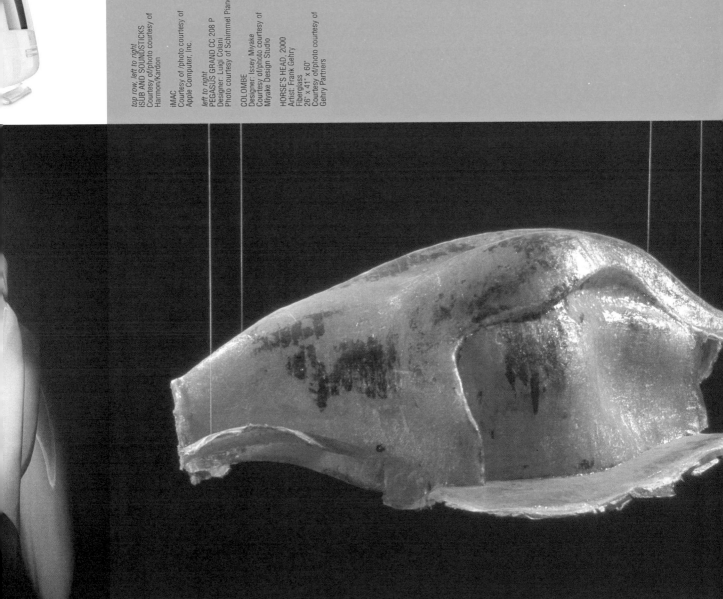

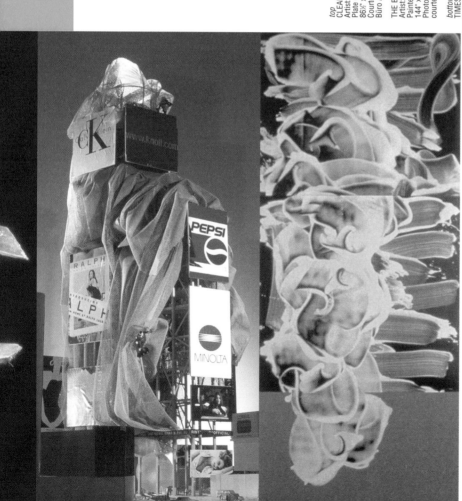

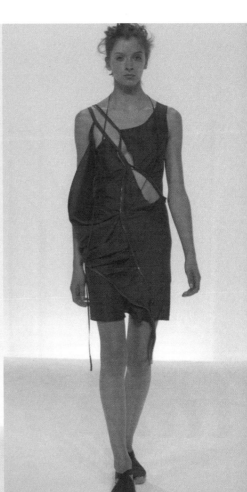

MAKING THE VISIBLE... VISIBLE...
JOSE OUBRERIE

Once upon a time, before Art as such was invented, so-called primitive civilizations produced magnificent objects for their daily use without knowing that they would end up as objects of admiration in our Museums.

The *Mood River* exhibition aims to reveal that such a chain of consistency and quality can still be identified today, from all-too-familiar objects we do not really see to objects of contemplation. Razors, pens, kayaks, and bicycles take their place, claim their recognition, get their revenge. Organized in different arrangements—clouds, vortices, schools—to produce astonishment and delectation, the shapes, colors, and charms of these things unfold along the full length of the galleries, where they are joined here and there by artworks to punctuate shared themes of form and surface.

In his films, Sergei Eisenstein longed "to bring the spectator to a state of ecstasy" and such was the ultimate goal assigned to the installation of *Mood River.* Its implementation in such a linear sequence of idiosyncratic galleries as found in Peter Eisenman's Wexner Center presented more than one opportunity for an analogy with the construction of a movie. To realize his search for "pathetic" effects in his filmic narratives, Eisenstein turned to extreme techniques of assembling and structuring images and sounds in disjoint and layered sequences; the spirit of these inventions proved an invaluable resource for our installation.

Mood River, too, has a storyline, a set of unfolding plots such as the "School of Fish," the bubbling reef of taillights, the "Cascade of Chairs," the beautifully shaped *Free Basin* and the cavernous rumors of sound it projects, the joyous Vortices. This curatorial narrative develops sequentially and rhythmically, favored by the cinematic disposition of the galleries along the interminable linear ramp of the center.

At the usual entrance to the exhibitions, on one side of a central wall, the disposition of the ramp reveals an ascending perspectival effect that emphasizes an "infinite-like" ending, while providing an understanding of the spatiality of the experience yet to come. Challenging the coherent ease of this linear ascent, the discomforting first gallery, a "cul-de-sac" on the other side of the central wall at the entry, acts as a spatially dividing device reminiscent of Ghirlandaio's *The Visitation*. To ensure the cinematic perception, it became necessary to resolve the existing physical discontinuity between the first gallery and the ramp, so a new stair and opening were inserted in the central wall to allow direct access to the ramp from the first gallery.

This reinterpretation of the perspectival effects that underscore the generation of the major spatial elements of this building—from the flattened outside portico to the triangularly shaped galleries (that act as visual cones)—set the stage for the installation. Such a strong architectural proposal forced us to recognize and reinstate, as far as possible, the original conditions of the building, reexposing to the visitors its intrinsic design quality, which allows it to become one of the exhibited artifacts as well their receptacle.

To plainly enforce the autonomy of both the receptacle and the *Mood River* exhibits, we had to renounce the usual "designs" of most such exhibitions. These generally evolve between two extremes: either skillfully nailing works on painted walls, hoping that their selection and their organization will suffice; or constructing an overwhelming apparatus negligent of the underlying architecture. Most often, spatial modifications by temporary partitions denature or obfuscate the understanding of the original architectural setting.

We established two principles. First, to best reveal and honor the container, only the selected artifacts were to be made visible, and consequently, the instrumentalization of their means of presentation had to be invisible. Then, to make the objects truly visible, not merely seen, we had to "deterritorialize" them, remove them from the habits of expectation, strip them of their familiarity. To that end, we turned to a familiar exercise used in every introductory drawing class, where the teacher turns the still-life subject matter such as a vase upside down, so that the students begin to see, pay attention to form, color, and surface, not to the vase as such. All of the installation set pieces and devices—fish, cloud, vortices, etc.—in *Mood River* are but elaborate versions of this exercise, with the added ambition of introducing a sense of mood and immersion to the deterritorializing experience. Thus, for example, the reef of taillights removes the forty-plus fixtures from the automobiles and tiles them into an undulating coral carpet. The viewer encounters these jewels in an entirely unfamiliar mode and, hopefully, discovers the intrinsic beauty and the brilliance of their individual design. The notable exception to this principle of deterritorialization is in our treatment of the artworks in the exhibition. Since art takes up for itself the task of deterritorialization, drawing close, reflective attention to itself, we installed it according to the artist's original intent.

Finally, like a film, the *Mood River* installation is the irreducible work of a skilled team, every member of which made unique and creative contributions. Without my close colleagues and friends exhibition designers Jim Scott, David Bamber, Ben Knepper, Pug Heller, lighting consultant John Bohuslawsky, and all the associate craftspeople and installers, there would be nothing to discuss. Ultimately, the *Mood River* installation design is a quest to fully realize an astonishing interplay between the container and its contents, altogether working diagrammatically as the intertwined spirals of DNA magically do. If, in any measure we succeeded, it is because we worked so memorably well together.

José Oubrerie, Installation Design Consultant for Mood River, *is a renowned architect and Professor in the Knowlton School of Architecture at The Ohio State University.*

FREE BASIN
Birch wood, metal supports
Courtesy of SIMPARCH
Photos: Tom van Endyne,
Matt Lynch

SKATEBOARDS *left to right*
FLIP ROWLEY HAND
FIRM BOB BURNQUIST NEW WAVE BB
Courtesy of/photos courtesy of
BLITZ Distribution

ALIEN WORKSHOP DANNY WAY CREEPS SERIES
ALIEN WORKSHOP CREEPS SERIES
Courtesy of/photos courtesy of
DNA Distribution

FIRM SPIDER NEW WAVE
HOOK-UPS POSSE
FIRM RAY GUN
Courtesy of/photos courtesy of
BLITZ Distribution

HABITAT O'CONNER
Courtesy of/photo courtesy of
DNA Distribution

BIKES *left to right*
SCHWINN ANDREW FARIS
"AZRAEL"
Courtesy of/photo
courtesy of Pacific Cycle

03 GEROLSTEINER TEAM
BIKE
Courtesy of/photo courtesy
of Klein Bicycles

MONOCOQUE USA
SR 2.0 24"
SR 71
WERKS DHR
Courtesy of/photos
courtesy of Haro Bicycle
Corporation

NO.1
PAINT BALL GUN

X AND Y AXIS
SERVO'S

ADJUSTABLE
BASE TUBE

PAINT BALL GUN
TRIGGER SERVO

BASE UNIT

NO.1

NO.2

NO.3

NO.4

Paint-Ball Robot
Paintants
Fabian Marcaccio

PROTRUDE, FLOW, 2001
Artists: Sachiko Kodama and Minako Takeno
Mixed media
Courtesy of/photo courtesy of
Sachiko Kodama and Minako Takeno
Photo: Yozo Takada

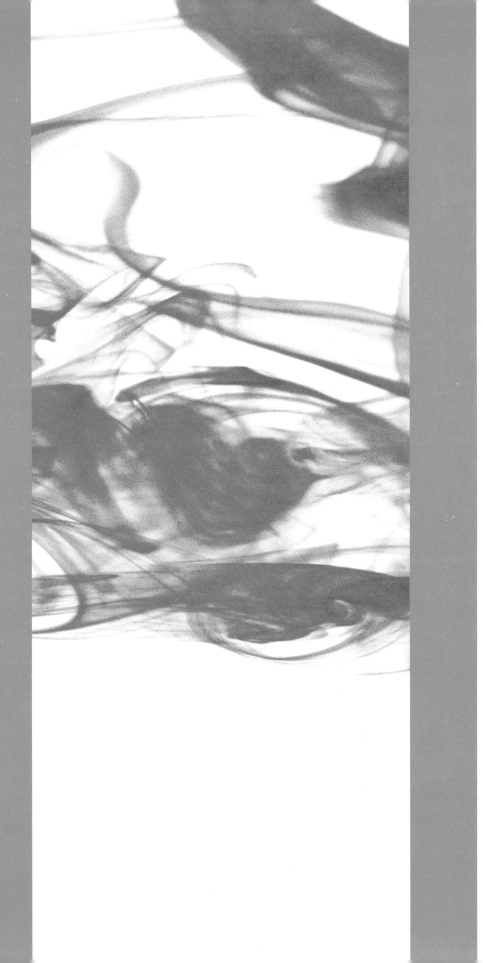

"…but what do such large loose baggy monsters, with their queer elements of the accidental and the arbitrary, artistically mean?"

In 1907, Henry James asked this question of *War and Peace* and kindred epic novels, his "baggy monster" since becoming the stock epithet for all sprawling projects that spill over the threshold of control, such as *Mood River.* Like the fragile walls of Gothic cathedrals propped up by flying buttresses and according to economics' inexorable law of diminishing returns, such monsters absorb more and more resources of every kind: time, energy, money, and most importantly, an exorbitant commitment from a large and varied cast of characters. For *Mood River,* most of these people felt like they were "just doing their job" and neither wanted nor expected explicit acknowledgment; but we, the curators, know that in the exaggerations of the show, there was no such thing for anyone involved as just doing a job. We want each and every one to know how much we remember and care, and how grateful we are for their efforts. Like ancient mariners, we will long tell all we encounter the innumerable tales—comic, dramatic, and tragic—that we have accumulated over the last two years, each of which stars a difference combination of our newfound friends, each of which stirs our heart again on the retelling.

Frankly, there is no way for us adequately to acknowledge the contributions so many have made. Our solution, inelegant at best, is to allow the Director's Preface, the image captions, and the lenders and donors lists to call attention to the majority of the generous people who made this exhibition possible. We hope you will read these with this additional burden in mind. Because these devices omit some and speak too insufficiently to the role of others, we call attention to a few in the hope that many, many more will know that our deep sense of gratitude embraces them all.

Our core curatorial team included *Jill Davis,* the Wexner Center's implacable exhibitions manager, and *Amy Schmersal, Joby Pottmeyer,* and *Rujuta Mody,* our student assistants. Jill's work in the field is already legendary, but few will know Amy, Joby, and

Rujuta. Suffice it to say that working with them transcended a positive professional experience. Their *esprit de corps,* cheerfulness, work ethic, energy, thoroughness, and intelligence inspired the two us. If these three are indicative of their generation, then we should just turn the world over to them now; they will make it a better place.

We thrived on an informal group of cool hunters who fed us key suggestions for the show. People like *Sonia Eram, Ben Nicholson, Suzie Attiwill, Karen Simonian* (who also serves as the Wexner Center press liaison), and especially *Eric Lynn, Greg Lynn, Eric Barkow,* and *Sherri Geldin* (that's right, she does a lot more than produce and direct). But if we mention them, we dare not neglect the pathfinders and trailblazers who first discovered most of the work in the exhibition, the army of *writers and editors of the art and design magazines* like *I.D., Wallpaper, Surface, One, the New York Times, Artforum, Art in America,* and *Flash Art,* who tirelessly scour the earth for all things interesting. And the Web and all those incredible people who put stuff on it, to whom we owe the debt of a thousand lives. And to the other *design curators* whose seminal shows at the Cooper-Hewitt, MoMA, and elsewhere set the stage for *Mood River,* not to mention the most courageous breed of all, the visionary retailers like *Murray Moss.*

Paola Antonelli and *Chee Pearlman* must be specially mentioned, so manifold was their advice, encouragement, and contribution. *Philip Johnson, Sanford Kwinter,* and *Sylvia Lavin* show up in the table of contents, but appear in this context for their cherished counsel. From catalogue to exhibition, *David Whitney* is nowhere to be found but everywhere to be felt, our guardian angel. We must violate our own vow not to call undo attention in these remarks to any one of our legion of gifted designers and artists, each deserving of a story in his or her own right, to note the special pleasures of working in the context of the exhibition with the Wexner Center's 2001–2 artist in residence, *Hussein Chalayan.*

Like messengers from the gods, a few appeared out of nowhere to shepherd us through one crisis or another, then disappeared as quickly. The made the impossible happen, they said, "no problem" when everyone else said, "no way": *Irving Lavin, Jennifer Frutchy, Chuck Helm, Mary McCann, Noel Harkey, Chris Nolte and the wonderful citizens of Storm Lake, Iowa, Bill Lantz, Keith Mendenhall, Omar Nobel and Annika MacVeigh, David Hudson,* and *Gayle Strege*, to cite a few. Each of these names represents a story too long and too rich to hint at here, so we fly their names only as a flag of thanks. Stop either of us in the gallery or on the street and let us tell one of the stories to you.

Virtually no one who works at the Wexner Center speaks to either of us at the moment, so this is our only chance to thank a few to represent the heroic efforts of all. Guest graphic designer *Patrick Li* worked shoulder to shoulder with Wexner Center editor *Ann Bremner* and senior graphic designer *Jeff Packard* and their team to extract late texts like stubborn teeth (including this one), pour over checklists, and lay out exhibitor-provided images and *Roman Sapecki's* commissioned photographs to pull off the miracle of this catalogue and the other ancillary graphics for the show.

In an equally heroic effort, guest installation designer *José Oubrerie* joined guest lighting consultant *John Bohuslawsky,* Wexner Center chief exhibition designer *James A. Scott*, designers *David Bamber, Ben Knepper,* and *Pug Heller* and their team of installers, and technical services manager *John Smith*, design engineer *Steve Jones*, and their team to conceive, design, and execute what amounts to a gigantic set piece. We can't thank any of them enough, mainly because they won't let us get near enough. As we write these words, most of them are holed up in a shop attaching thousands of strings to toothbrushes, cutlery, and chairs, cursing each of our names with each knot. I guess a few are still outside trying to shoulder the seventy-five foot, four ton turbine blade onto its stand.

Think about our registration department, *Jennifer Roy* and *Melissa Donovan* under the regal leadership of *Joan Hendricks*. They have to ship, inspect, and insure the proper white-glove handling of each and everything that comes into the center for exhibition. Now, think about 600 toothbrushes, 50 taillights, art and furniture from five continents, stuff being stuffed every day through the mail slot, a ceiling fan from Australia, bicycles and skateboards galore. Need we say more?

So many on the Wexner Center staff did so much that to mention one is to neglect five equally deserving. For every person who spent too much time on this show, someone else like *Steve Hunt* took up the slack on another. These efforts also count to us and for us. *Beth Fisher* and *Jeff Byars* led their group in the fundraising effort, their nonstop enthusiasm for the show truly buoying our spirits. *Patricia Trumps* and her staff in the education department arranged a schedule of visiting lectures and expert performances to surpass both in depth and interest the exhibition itself. Their work with *Amanda Ault* from our film/video department to produce the *Mood River* boards and bikes conference and demonstration is particularly exciting. *Kris Flaherty*, Wexner Center special events coordinator, is in the midst of planning the opening from hell, with hoards of guests descending from every planet, each expecting individual attention. Amazingly, she will pull it off; she always does. Numerous others also went above and beyond for *Mood River,* among them, *Misty Dickerson,* our receptionist, and *everyone at our delivery dock/mail room and in our business office.*

We save our penultimate thoughts for *Gretchen Metzelaars*, director of Wexner Center administration, *Joel Schaefer*, our head of security, and *Patrick Maughan*, security liaison with the university. Almost everything about this show, from floating knives to open skateboarding in the gallery, gave them nightmares and sent up innumerable red flags on campus. Without compromising the safety and security of our visitors or the items on display, they always found a way to help us realize our dreams, all the while keeping the naysaying wolves at bay at much personal expense. We know it and appreciate it.

Our final and ultimate thought, of course, goes to *Sherri.*

ANNETTA MASSIE AND JEFFREY KIPNIS

AdHoc Entwicklung and Vertrieb GmbH
Aeromax
Agape SRL
Aliantedizioni
Alias Spa
Apple Computer, Inc.
Applied Concepts
Artemide
Artitudes Designs
Bang & Olufsen
Beauté Prestige International
Becton Dickinson
Bell Sports
Bernhardt Design
BikeSource
BLITZ Distribution
Blu Dot
Bluesquare
BMW of North America
BOLT
Boum Design
Brookstone Company
Brown Jordan
Büro Anthony Cragg
Burton Snowboards
Byers Dublin Dodge
Byers Imports on Hamilton
Canadian Centre for Architecture, Montreal
Cannondale Corporation
Caran d'Ache of Switzerland
Casabella
Hussein Chalayan
Chesrown Oldsmobile GMC, KIA
Ane Christensen
Colgate Palmolive
Colibri
CP Company
A. T. Cross Company
Danese Milano
Dave Gill Pontiac-GMC
Deluxe SF Distribution
Dennis Mitsubishi Inc

Designor OyAb, Hackman Tools Helsinki, Finland
DNA Distribution
Donna Karan Cosmetics Company
Dornbracht GmbH
DQ
Dwindle Distribution
Dyson Ltd
Ed Potter, Inc
Edra Spa
Ethentica
Euro-Pro Corporation
FibreFlex
Fisher-Price
Fiskars Consumer Products, Inc.
Flex-Dex
Flowlab LLC
Forms+Surfaces
Foscarini USA
Foundation 33
Galyan's
Gary Fisher Bicycles, Inc.
Gehry Partners
Germain Toyota
Giant Bikes
The Gillette Company
GlaxoSmithKline
Gordon & Smith Surfboards
Timothy Grannis
Fratelli Guzzini
Hammacher Schlemmer
Harmon/Kardon
Haro Bicycle Corporation
Hitachi Power Tools
Hoffman Bikes
Enlai Hooi
Hopf + Wortmann, Munich
Huffy Bicycles
Immke Crestview Cadillac
ISI North America
Jorg Hysek
Kartell
Kikkerland

Klein Bicycles
Sachiko Kodama and Minako Takeno
Korban/Flaubert
Harri Koshinen
Koziol Geschenkartikel GmbH
LeMond Bicycles
L'Equip
Lexon, distributed by Zona Alta Projects
Lindsay Acura
Luminair, Inc.
Greg Lynn
Macho Products, Inc.
Fabian Marcaccio
Marutomi
Mathmos Ltd
Max Protetch Gallery
Metrokane
MidWestern Auto Group
Miyake Design Studio
Mono Tabletop
Moorhead & Moorhead
Musee d'Art Moderne Grand-Duc Jean, Luxembourg
Museo Alessi
Museum of Fine Arts, Houston
The Museum of Modern Art, New York
Nelson Auto Group
Never Summer
Chris Neville
Ben Nicholson
OrangeX
OXO International
PaceWildenstein, New York
Pacific Cycle
Giovanni Pagnotta
Parks Products
Chee Pearlman
Perception, Inc.
Anthony Podesta, Washington, D.C.
Polyline
Mike Portman
R+D Design
Karim Rashid

Rosendahl A/S, Denmark
The Saatchi Gallery, London
Sailworks, R+D Loft
Salter Housewares
Sanford Corporation
San Francisco Museum of Modern Art
Sarah Schwartz
Sector 9
Sensa by Willat
Servo
SheafferPen, Division of Bic USA Inc.
Shiseido
SIMPARCH
Smith & Hawken
Snowcrash
Sointu USA Incorporated
Kivi Sotamaa and Markus Holmsten
Frank Stella
Stone Island
City of Storm Lake, Iowa, and the Storm Lake Chamber of Commerce
Tony Stuart
Swingline, a division of ACCO Brands Inc
The Terence Conran Shop
Terminal-NYC
Ansel Thompson
Tiffany & Co.
Tombow
Trek Bicycles
Tripod Design
Tumyeto Corporation
Bob Turner
Unilever Home and Personal Care
Valli & Valli USA Inc
VISA VERSA
Vitra, Inc
Malte Wagenfeld
Watermark Designs
Westerville Bike
Wills Wing
Wiss
xO

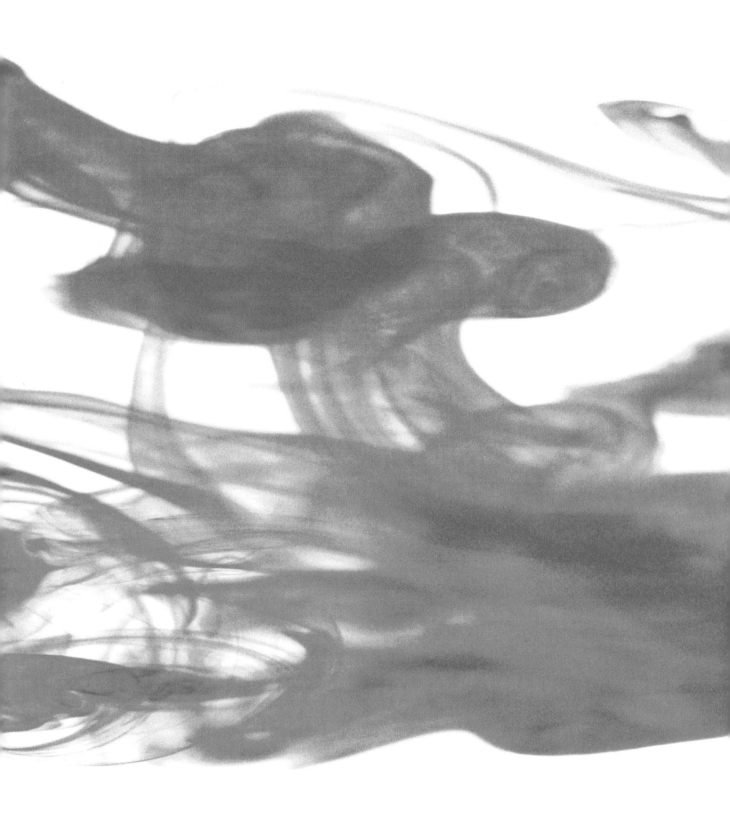

DATE DUE
